D1645607

The Royal Coat of Arms of Her Majesty Queen Elizabeth the Queen Mother

The QUEEN MOTHER *and Family* AT HOME IN CAITHNESS

Queen Elizabeth the Queen Mother on her annual summer visit to the Mey Games, Caithness

The QUEEN MOTHER *and Family* AT HOME IN CAITHNESS

Produced and Designed
by
CLIVE RICHARDS

Published by
North of Scotland Newspapers Limited
Home of the
JOHN O'GROAT JOURNAL & CAITHNESS COURIER
42 Union Street, Wick, Caithness, Scotland

ISBN 1 871704 03 0

Typeset by North of Scotland Newspapers Limited,
42 Union Street, Wick, Caithness, Scotland.
Printed by Highland News Group Limited, Henderson Road, Inverness, Scotland.
The typeface used for text in this book is 10 point Times Roman.
Printed on Trucote Velvet 135 gm².

COVER FRONT: A Birthday Portrait of Her Majesty Queen Elizabeth The Queen Mother with her favourite corgis, Billy and Bee, in the privacy of her Caithness home.

FRONTISPIECE: One of the first official photographs of the Queen Mother at the Castle of Mey.

COVER BACK: The Castle of Mey in all its floodlit splendour.

ACKNOWLEDGEMENTS

Unless otherwise stated, the photographs in this book are by John Adams. Additional photographs are reproduced by kind permission of the following: Northern Studios, Wick, Pages 1 and 20; Times Newspapers Limited, Page 9; The Glasgow Herald, Pages 10, 11, 13, 16, 17 and 18, Aberdeen Journals Limited, Pages 14 and 15.

The Publishers gratefully acknowledge the assistance of Nan Budge, Achalone, Halkirk and Caithness District Council for the use of photographic prints by John Adams on Pages 32 to 35 inclusive and Pages 112 to 128 inclusive, respectively.

John Adams at work: (Left) Photographed by his daughter Shona, at the Mey Sheep Dog Trials in August 1964. For the pictur behind the picture please turn to Page 131.

The Highland Show Inverness 1947: King George VI and Queen Elizabeth accompanied by Princess Margaret (partly seen) with Sir Donald Cameron of Locheil. (Centre) Appointed Lord Lieutenant of Inverness in 1939

A Portrait of John Adams. Photographed by Thomas Pratt in the Highland Studio Pitlochry 1970.

Introduction

THE photographic record of the 1950s and 60s — now faded pages contained in the old files of the *John O'Groat Journal,* newspapers — bears testimony to the work, skill and artistry of one time Caithness photographer John Cyril Percy Adams. Now in his 79th year, John and his wife Mary enjoy idyllic retirement in the town of Ramsay on the Isle of Man, where, in April 1989, I spent two unforgettable days in their company and was granted the privilege of sharing through John's photographs, Caithness life of not so long ago. Sadly, I was soon to learn that the vast majority of the thousands of photographic negatives of the faces and places of Caithness, which John had amassed during his 20 years as a photographer in the far north, had been destroyed. Hopefully, many of the original photographic prints will have weathered the test of time in the safe keeping of family albums or framed with pride on numerous walls, sideboards and mantelpieces throughout the county.

Born in Eltham, London, on 19th October 1911, the young John Adams entered the world of photography through the RAF photographic school, Farnborough, in the late 1920s. In those days photography was a new branch of the service and the use of bulky 5″ x 4″ glass plates and IR17 air cameras was the order of the day.

In 1932 John was sent to the North-West Frontier of India on reconnaissance missions over the Himalayas, returning to the United Kingdom in 1939. The RAF photographic section was of vital importance to the war effort and at its outbreak he was commissioned and despatched to France with the latest mobile photographic unit comprising 18 men. The unit had at its disposal all British air cameras which used 5″ x 4″ cut film and could process and print on the spot. With a detachment of number 2 Army Co-operation Squadron, the unit landed at Abbeville in France. On reaching Lille in Belgium some months later, they successfully captured a German tank, the fuel from which enabled them to proceed to the coast.

Unaware of the serious situation taking place on the beaches of Dunkirk, they eventually reached west of Nantes, where to their relief a British ferry boat was berthed in the harbour. The boat was duly commandeered for service and they were able to put their precious mobile unit aboard and get some much needed rest.

During the D-Day preparations in 1944, John was sent from RAF Headquarters, Bracknell, to St. James Square, London. It was here that a special unit was set up to print 6ft photographic maps for use in connection with the second front. Surrounded with barbed wire, the unit was so secret that John Adams every movement was shadowed by the security services to prevent enemy agents obtaining vital information which could lead to the precise location of the front.

Following the successful D-Day landings, John was transferred to Dalmore House in Ross-shire, to take charge of the RAF photographic section. He met his wife Mary in Inverness, who at that time was a WREN at the Royal Naval Hospital, Invergordon. When peace was declared they married in Mary's home town of Bristol.

In 1946 John resigned his commission, only to be told by his best man, Doctor Freddie Anderson, that he would be invalided out of the service on the grounds of ill health. Freddie advised John to move to Caithness to aid his recuperation in the "Champagne Air." Never one to ignore good advice, John set up as a photographer in Wick the same year. Trading as the Caithness Studio, he acquired the old photographic studio in River Street which had been vacated by photographer J. G. Humphrey. Humphrey only used daylight lighting for his portraits so John had to set about the complete modernisation of the premises. Subsequently, he introduced flash photography for weddings which made him the fashionable photographer of the day.

Both he and his old friend David Oag — Editor in those days of the *John O'Groat Journal* — helped keep Caithness in the forefront of the national news.

Despite the fact John Adams was a keen member of the Old Stagers Rifle Team and represented them on many occasions, it was never his intention to stay in Wick for more than a year or two, but he found the people so friendly and his photographic services in such demand that he stayed and prospered for 20 years, after which he moved to Pitlochry trading as the Highland Studio from where, in 1976, he retired to the Isle of Man.

John and Mary have two children both born in Wick. Daughter Shona, now married, works at a secretarial post in London and son Marcus, also married, is a pilot with British Airways on the latest 747-400 Boeing jets.

John Adams greatest honour was to be asked by the Queen Mother to take photographs at the Castle of Mey. These and many more memorable photographs contained within this book, rekindle an era in which the people of Caithness can share with pride in this, a celebration of Her Majesty Queen Elizabeth The Queen Mother's 90th Birthday.

Clive Richards 1990.

The story of the Queen Mother's new home and why she chose it

The story of the Queen Mother's choice of Barrogill Castle, which she renamed the Castle of Mey, is as romantic as that of the historic keep itself.

It arose partly from Her Majesty's desire to find a retreat far away from the pageantry of Royal life in London, partly from her instinct for scenic beauty and her love of fine architecture.

The Queen Mother bought her Castle of Mey in August, 1952. Two months earlier, when she was beginning to recover from the pain of the late King's death and found the number of her public engagements diminishing, the Queen Mother got into a Viking of the King's Flight and flew to Wick Airport where she was met by Commander and Lady Vyner, of the House of the Northern Gate, Dunnet Head.

On the thirty-mile drive by coast-road from Wick to Thurso, the Vyner's car passed a 16th century building called Barrogill Castle.

Like all Caithness Castles, which were built for defence rather than grandeur, it was small and compact. Its square facade and corbelled turrets seemed in good repair and this caught the Queen Mother's eye.

"It's been up for sale for months," said Lady Vyner, nodding towards Barrogill.

STOP THE CAR

"Stop the car a moment, please," said the Queen Mother.

She studied the castle with growing interest and then turned and asked excitedly: "Do you think it would suit me?"

Lady Vyner was not sure. In the days when it had been owned by the Earls of Caithness, Edward VII and Queen Alexandra as Prince and Princess of Wales had stayed there. But Lady Vyner knew that although its exterior was intact its interior had been badly mauled when it was used as a wartime billet for coast defence troops.

The Queen Mother, however, remained interested. A few days later she went to look it over.

The castle, which took 22 years to build, was completed in 1589. It was begun by George, 4th Earl of Caithness, who died before the work was finished, and it remained in the hands of his descendants for more than 300 years until it was sold to the 14th Earl. Now, the Queen Mother found its owners were Captain and Mrs Imbert-Terry, who no longer wished to keep it up.

There were no bathrooms, no electric light and no central heating. The Imbert-Terrys lived in only a few of its 30 rooms. They bathed in a Victorian hip bath, their illumination came from oil lamps and candles and their heat came from peat fires in the massive open grates.

But the Queen Mother saw in little Barrogill the possibilities of home that was not too big, a home she could fill with the flowers an bright chintzes she had always adored, yet not too small for th dignity of a sovereign's wife.

A HOBGOBLIN'S FASTNESS

From the outside Barrogill might look like a hobgoblin's fastnes but inside it could look like a fairy castle. As she toured its room with the Imbert-Terry's, she picked up souvenirs of Barrogill' lamplit past, oddments unwanted by buyers who came to the 14t Earl's auction, trinkets and pictures which gave her an insight int the personalities of those who had lived there before.

There was, for instance, the white parasol, which had belonge to Lady Fanny, the 14th Earl's daughter.

This one had come from Spain where its delicate fringe had bee used to hide a pair of lovely eyes and to show them. A Spanish Duk had wanted Lady Fanny's hand, but she rejected him. It is said Lad Fanny sometimes regretted her decision and was to be seen sittin under her parasol and dreaming of the golden sandstone walls of castle in Spain.

The Queen Mother inspected the staircase leading out of th main hall and perhaps visualised the Earls of centuries agc standing at the top in the flaming tartan of the Sinclair dress tartan receiving guests amid the glitter of buckled shoe, the clink c jewelled claymore and the strains of the fiddlers in the minstre gallery.

"THE PRIMROSE LADY"

There was at Barrogill, they said, a ghost called "The Primros Lady". It was the spirit of an early Earl's daughter who had fallen i love with a ploughboy and was locked up for weeks in a garret t forget her folly. Finally, she jumped to her death against the stone of the courtyard far below. Now she is said to walk the corridors c Barrogill with that same faintly mysterious smile on her face whic makes the portrait of her so magnetic.

There was a new ghost too. During the last world war, a piper i the Black Watch billeted in the castle was found shot dead.

They say he slow marches up and down the battlements playin "The Flowers of the Forest" and that every time he is seen, th plaster, which plugs his bullet hole in the wall, falls out.

Out in the 50 acres of ground, the Queen Mother was delighte by the high walls which enclose sections of the garden and mak protected bowers where it is possible to hide from the wind.

There is only one thing the Queen Mother did not like abou Barrogill — its name. And so she changed it to the Castle of Mey

Barrogill Castle: Renamed the Castle of Mey by Her Majesty the Queen Mother

The Queen Mother arrives at Wick Airport. She smiles to the waiting crowd as she sets foot in Caithness for the first time (16th June 1952). Her Majesty, accompanied by the Hon Mrs Mulholland, Lady-in-Waiting (Left), is met by her host and hostess, Commander C.G. Vyner and Lady Vyner.

Our Royal Visitor

Caithness has been honoured and privileged by the presence of Her Majesty Queen Elizabeth the Queen Mother who came north for a four-day private stay with personal friends at Dunnet. As far as history records, this was the first visit of a Queen to the county.

The Queen Mother has been the guest of Commander C. G. Vyner and Lady Doris Vyner, a personal friend, at the House of the Northern Gate, Dunnet. The house is situated on Dwarick Head — a white, prominent building overlooking the sea.

Her Majesty arrived at Wick Airport on Monday afternoon, 16th June, in a Viking of the King's Flight. Thousands of people assembled at the aerodrome to see the Queen Mother.

The three burgh schools closed early so that pupils could attend at the airport. The children from the primary schools, Wick North and Pulteneytown Academy, marched there in classes under the charge of their teachers, while the High School pupils paraded also. Many of the children carried flags.

The first sign of the approaching aircraft was a loud cheer from the school children, and a few minutes later — at 4.35 p.m. — the plane touched down on the landing ground.

A cool north-westerly wind swept the airfield but, as if in deference to the Royal visitor, the sun shone for the first time for many days in this coldest June weather experienced for years.

An enthusiastic cheer greeted Her Majesty as she appeared framed in the doorway of the plane. She was accompanied by the Hon. Mrs Mulholland, Lady-in-Waiting.

Commander Vyner and Lady Vyner went forward to meet the Queen Mother. Just then, the crowds broke from the ordered queue and surged round to get a closer look at Her Majesty. Smiling and waving to the people, the Royal visitor made her way forward to the waiting car. She stopped and spoke to one or two schoolchildren near her, saying how pleased she was to see them.

When Queen Elizabeth the Queen Mother arrived in Wick to begin her visit to the Northern Towns, she captivated everyone with her endearing smile.

JUNE 1952

Thurso gives a warm welcome

At noon on Tuesday, 17th June, 1952, the Queen Mother arrived at Thurso to inspect the quick-freeze factory, owned by St. Clair Fisheries, Ltd., of which Commander Vyner is managing director. Over 70 persons, mostly all women — some being part-time workers — are engaged in the factory, which is a new post-war venture in Thurso.

The factory processes crabs and lobsters for manufacturing firms in the South, and also fillets and quick freezes white fish.

The weather was warm and sunny, and a large crowd of people had gathered outside the factory to await Her Majesty's arrival.

The Queen Mother was accompanied by Commander and Lady Vyner. Mr John Graham, solicitor, Wick, secretary of the company, Mr A. Macdonald, factor, and Provost John Sinclair were in the party during the inspection of the factory. The Royal visitor spent some time on the premises and showed a great interest in the work being carried on. She spoke to a number of the women who explained the processing of the shell fish.

On leaving the factory, Her Majesty, accompanied by Provost Sinclair and the rest of the party, walked across the harbour quay, smiling to the acknowledgment of the cheering crowd. She stood for some time on the quay speaking to the Provost, discussing with him the fishing industry, in which she showed great interest. She seemed to be enjoying too, the view across the river with Thurso Castle in the background. At the time, salmon fishers were busy at work in the river estuary.

A small Terrier dog, wishing to show his loyalty, went forward and placed his forepaws against the Queen Mother as if to say, "I am here too". Her Majesty knelt to pat the little dog.

Returning to her car, the Queen Mother got a rousing send-off from the crowd and especially the factory workers who had come out to cheer.

The main streets of Thurso were crowded as the car drove through. The people gave the Royal visitor an enthusiastic reception. The car stopped at the shop of J. Miller Calder, furniture and antique dealers, in Traill Street, one of the oldest established businesses in Caithness. The Queen Mother spent some time in the shop, being received by one of the partners in the firm, Miss B. Calder. Her Majesty made a number of purchases. She expressed surprise at finding an antique shop of this type so far North.

After leaving Thurso the Queen Mother went on to Halkirk, and there the pupils of Halkirk Secondary School left their classes shortly before 1 p.m. so that they could be down on the road when the Queen Mother passed. Her Majesty waved to the cheering children as the car drove slowly along. Shortly before this the weather broke and there was a brief storm of rain and hailstones, after which the sun shone again.

"I am here too", the little dog seems to say as the Queen Mother talks with Provost John Sinclair of Thurso during her visit to the Quick Freeze Factory.

Queen Mother climbs 70 steps to see the sunset over the Atlantic

In the afternoon the Queen Mother made a surprise visit to Duncansby Head Lighthouse, accompanied by Commander and Lady Vyner. She spent half-an-hour in the lighthouse being shown over it by the principal keeper, Mr Alexander C. Dishon. The assistant keeper is Mr R. Macdonald. The weather was ideal at the time and Her Majesty got a splendid view of the surrounding scenery. She told Mr Dishon that this was only the second time that she had ever visited a lighthouse, and said that lighthouse keepers were doing a vital job. She complimented the keepers on the condition of the lighthouse. The Queen Mother and her friends had a picnic lunch in the grounds outside the lighthouse.

Dunnet Lighthouse

Along with her host and hostess, the Queen Mother paid a visit to Dunnet Head Lighthouse on Tuesday evening and watched the sun set over the Atlantic.

Her arrival at the lighthouse at about 9pm was quite unexpected, and nobody could have been more surprised than Mr John Scott, principal keeper, when he realised whom the visitor was.

"The lighthouse lamp was not lit then and I was on duty outside when I saw the car arrive", said Mr Scott. "I did not know it was the Queen Mother until she was about 40 yards from me, so you can imagine my surprise. My wife and assistant keepers and their families were introduced to the Royal visitor, after which she climbed the 70-step stair to the top of the lighthouse. She was very interested in the whole operation of the station.

"After signing the visitors' book and descending from the tower, and seeing the fog signal plant", said Mr Scott, "the Queen Mother, who had apparently seen my two children at the door — they had been in bed but rose again on hearing the news — specially asked if she could see them. By that time they had dressed, and she chatted with them before leaving."

Tuesday night being one of the clearest and most pleasant this summer, the view from Dunnet was magnificent and the Queen Mother expressed her delight with it. She and her host and hostess stopped for some time after leaving the lighthouse, and watched the sun set over the Altantic.

Dunnet Head Lighthouse

Wick turns out to greet the Queen Mother

Large crowds press round Royal Car

The people of the Royal Burgh of Wick gave the Queen Mother a royal welcome when she visited the town on hursday, 19th June, 1952. Her Majesty was due to arrive at ne Town Hall at 11.45 a.m. Long before then a large crowd ad assembled in Bridge Street.

When the car conveying the Royal visitor drove up there as loud and prolonged cheering. A square in front of the own building had been roped off. A red carpet was laid out n the street and led into the hall.

The entrance to the hall and the stairways leading to the hambers were artistically decorated with beautiful flowers, s was also the chambers. The trim tidy appearance of the own buildings externally, and the decorative effect inside ere most befitting to the occasion.

Along with the Queen Mother were Commander and ady Vyner and Mrs Robert Somerset, a personal friend.

Her Majesty was received by Miss Bessie Leith, Wick's irst woman Provost, who was accompanied by her fellow nagistrates — Bailies David Nicol, John Macleod and Robert J. McRobbie — and Miss Jess M. Page, town clerk Mrs Jess M. Campbell, retired depute director of Caithness District Council), the first woman to hold full-time office as own clerk in Scotland.

Entering the hall, the party went upstairs to the Council chambers where the Queen Mother was presented to the Councillors and also to Sheriff R. N. Levitt and Rev. P. F. C. Black, Wick Old Parish Church, representing the law and the clergy.

Her Majesty showed special interest in a Coronation clock displayed in the hall. It is the property of Mr D. Cormack, watchmaker, Wick, and was made in 1937 during the Coronation Year of the Queen Mother.

The Royal visitor then signed the visitors' book with a special quill pen given for the occasion. She sat in the Provost's chair, a beautifully designed carved piece of furniture which is 106 years old. It was presented to the council by Mr John Bruce, Tarool, Watten. The chair is made from a rafter of dark oak from Kirkwall Cathedral.

Afterwards, the Queen Mother remained in the chambers for some time speaking to some of the councillors. She discussed with Bailie John Macleod the town's staple industry, the fishing, and also referred to the storm damage in the county caused by the hurricane last January, expressing sympathy for those who had suffered loss, particularly the farming community.

On her way out of the hall, Her Majesty stopped to chat with a few of the guests assembled in the entrance.

Below: Almost the entire town turned out to greet the Queen Mother when she called on Wick's Lady Provost — Miss Bessie Leith. The large crowd pressed round the Royal Car, and it required the best efforts of the police to clear a pathway for the Royal visitor.

Overleaf: (June 1952). Provost Bessie Leith greeted the Queen Mother with a gracious curtsey as she arrived at Wick Town Hall.

The Queen Mother signs the visitors' book in the Council Chambers at Wick.

School children walk miles to see the Queen Mum

On leaving the Town Hall, the)ueen Mother was presented with bouquet of pink carnations by 'rovost Leith. She expressed to the 'rovost the pleasure which her visit ɔ Wick had given, and she special-y commented on the spontaneous velcome of the large crowd. Her Majesty asked particularly about he children and said she was leased to see so many of them gain.

At every village and hamlet on he 30-mile route to Berriedale, ɔcal inhabitants, including the upils of the various schools, athered at the roadside to cheer he Royal visitor. Some walked everal miles from their homes to he road. For instance Miss McI-or, teacher at Tannach, and her ix pupils walked three miles to 'hrumster Post Office, where the upils of Thrumster and Whaligoe chools were among the crowd.

Pupils of Lybster Junior Secon-ary School paraded from the chool, under the charge of their eachers, to the main road opposite he Portland Arms Hotel, and ɔined the crowd of people there, s did pupils of other schools on the oute. At each village the Queen Aother's car slowed down and she vaved acknowledgment to their nthusiastic cheers.

At Berriedale, the Royal visitor ad lunch with the Duke and)uchess of Portland at Langwell Iouse and visited the beautiful ardens before returning to Wick y the same route. Many who were nable to see her on the southward un were waiting to cheer her on he return journey. At Latheron a re-arranged telephone message vas received when the car had assed Dunbeath on its way north, nd in about a quarter of an hour ractically the entire population urned out again for a second limpse of the Queen Mother.

Few people in Wick observed he car driving through the streets n its return from Berriedale. On he way to Dunnet the Queen Aother made an unexpected visit o Keiss. The car drove slowly lown the length of the street and ack to the main road. The villa-ers were soon aware of their Royal visitor's presence and came locking to the scene. Amusement vas caused when two-year-old Wil-iam Bain, son of Mr Wm. Bain, us driver, Keiss, toddled forward owards the car. Her Majesty miled and waved as she passed on.

A Queen's Escort: Provost Leith followed by Jess Page escorts Her Majesty as she leaves the Town Hall, Wick.

Her Majesty smiles to the cheering crowd after receiving a bouquet of pink carnations from Bessie Leith, accompanied by Je. Page, on the right of the picture, and other members of the party.

Wick children sang, "Will Ye No' Come Back Again"

The Queen Mother returned to Balmoral on Friday afternoon, 18th June, flying from Wick Airport in a Viking of the King's Flight.

A large crowd gathered at the Aerodrome in the afternoon to see the Royal visitor's departure. The Queen Mother, who motored from Dunnet, arrived at the Airport shortly before four o'clock. She was accompanied by Commander and Lady Vyner, Mrs Robert Somerset and Lady Jean Rankin, Lady-in-Waiting. Her Majesty got a rousing cheer from the crowd and waved in acknowledgment from the car.

She was received by Commodore J. G. Murray, Divisional Controller of Civil Aviation (Scottish Division). Chief Constable W. K. Cormack was present also.

Wick children sang, "Will ye no' come back again." as the Queen Mother boarded the 'plane.

As the 'plane moved forward to the runway, the Queen Mother was seen waving to the crowd from the rear port window. At that moment, the children broke from the queue and ran several hundred yards to a vantage point on the runway to get a last glimpse of the Royal visitor as the 'plane soared gracefully out of sight.

"Lovely county"

The warm and enthusiastic reception which the Caithness people gave to the Queen Mother wherever she appeared in the county so impressed Her Majesty that she wrote to Provost Miss Bessie Leith expressing her appreciation.

Provost Leith has received the following letter from Marion Hyde, Lady-inWaiting to the Queen Mother:

"I am commanded by Queen Elizabeth the Queen Mother to write and convey to you Her Majesty's appreciation and pleasure at the wonderful welcome given to her last Thursday by the townspeople of Wick, and to say how much Queen Elizabeth enjoyed her visit to the Town House.

"The warmth and enthusiasm of the children who greeted Her Majesty on her arrival and departure from Wick Airfield will always remain a happy memory of Queen Elizabeth's visit to Caithness."

John O'Groats Jetty 1952: In an interview with the John O'Groat Journal, Commander Vyner was asked what Her Majesty thought of Caithness. "She thought it absolutely lovely and could not have wished for better".

AUGUST 1952

Queen Mother's visit to Caithness

Attends Church Service at Dunnet

During a four-day private visit to Caithness — the second within two months — Queen Elizabeth the Queen Mother attended Divine worship in Dunnet Church at noon on Sunday 17th June. Later, she returned south by road to Balmoral.

The Queen Mother came North from Balmoral for a private visit to Dunnet to reside with Commander C. G. and Lady Doris Vyner, with whom she stayed on her first visit to the county last June.

The Royal visitor, who had motored from Balmoral, was accompanied by Lady Delia Peel, Lady-in-Waiting.

On Friday, the Queen Mother picnicked at St. John's Point, overlooking the Pentland Firth. The weather was favourable, and Stroma Island stood out clearly in the near distance. Along with the Queen Mother were her host and hostess and Lady Delia Peel.

The Royal visitor visited North Sutherland and had a picnic at Strathy. Again she was accompanied by her Lady-in-Waiting and Commander and Lady Vyner.

The Queen Mother worshipped in Dunnet Church on Sunday. She motored from the House of the Northern Gate, the home of Commander and Lady Vyner, who accompanied her along with Lady Delia Peel, Mr Henry Vyner (son of Commander and Lady Vyner) and Lady Arabella Stuart.

It was a beautiful day — the best that the Royal visitor had had while in Caithness — and there was a large congregatio composed mostly of the local community, others fro surrounding districts and visitors on holiday in the area.

The Queen Mother was received at the front door of th church by Rev. Alexander M. Gordon who has bee minister at Dunnet for 10 years.

The service opened with the singing of Psalm 100. Prais was led by 76-year-old Mr William Dunnet, Corsback Dunnet, who has been precentor in the church for 54 year The organist was Mrs E. Mackenzie, Dunnet.

An impressive service was conducted by Mr Gordo whose inspiring address was based on the text "For I am th Lord that healeth thee" (Exodus XV, 26).

After the Benediction, the congregation sang the Nation Anthem.

On leaving the church, the Queen Mother said to M Gordon that she was sorry that she was leaving Caithnes that day. The Royal visitor left for the south in the earl afternoon.

Historic Church

Dunnet Church is one of the three oldest parish churche in Caithness still in use. The tower was built in pre-Reformation days and the church records date back to 1540.

(Rev. Timothy Pont, the map-maker, was minister o Dunnet Church from 1601 to 1610).

The House of the Northern Gate, Dunnet Head; Home of Commander and Lady Vyner, where the Queen Mother stayed on numerous occasions before taking up residence in The Castle of Mey. This photograph was taken after the house was converted into a residential hotel in the early 1970s.

AUGUST 1952

A Royal Residence in Caithness

Queen Mother buys Barrogill

It was disclosed officially on Monday, 25th August, that Queen Elizabeth the Queen Mother had purchased Barrogill Castle as a summer residence. The building, which suffered roof damage during the January hurricane, is already under repair.

Barrogill Castle, first known as the Castle of Mey, believed to be 400 years old, is one of the ancient seats of the Earls of Caithness. James, the 14th Earl, was the last of the family to occupy it.

For the past 20 years the castle and surrounding estates have been in the possession of Captain F. B. Imbert-Terry, who bought the property from Mrs Gerold, whose first husband, Mr Heathcote Sinclair, succeeded to it after the death of the last Earl. Mr Heathcote, who later added Sinclair to his name, was a friend of the Earl.

Recently, most of the estate was sold to farmers and other tenants by Captain Imbert-Terry.

The policies, including the gardens, extend to over 50 acres. There are over 30 rooms in the castle.

Situated only a few hundred yards from the shore, the castle overlooks the Pentland Firth. It is seven miles from John O'Groats, 13 from Thurso and 20 from Wick.

Royal visitors to Barrogill in 1876 were the Prince and Princess of Wales, who each planted a tree in the grounds.

No surprise

The purchase of Barrogill Castle by the Queen Mother did not come as a surprise to the people of Caithness. When she came to Caithness last June for the first time the Queen Mother visited the castle on several occasions, and on her return to the county in mid-August she again went to see the castle. When she first saw the building in June, the Queen Mother immediately took a fancy to it and later made up her mind to buy it.

County's Attractions

The following appeared in the "Scotsman" on 26th August, 1952, in the popular feature "A Scotsman's Log":

The Queen Mother could not very easily have chosen on the mainland, a summer home further away from London than Barrogill Castle in Caithness. Those who do not know the most northern mainland county may think of Caithness as a bleak and desolate county and may wonder why the Queen Mother should have chosen a summer residence in such a remote part of the world.

Bleak and desolate Caithness may be, but it is a county which tends to get under one's skin the more one sees it. After it has chugged up the valley of the Helmsdale River, the train runs for miles over tawny moors with low rolling horizons broken only by occasional cottages. What trees there are, are usually gnarled, small and stunted.

Any sense of a sombre and forbidding landscape is soon banished by the vast arc of sky, the rugged coastline and the great sweep of the sea with its racing tides and foam-girt skerries. Light seems to take on a new and refreshing quality as it plays on the Caithness moors, and the air has a wine-like caress when the sun shines and the wind blows.

Superb vista

Barrogill Castle is near the little village of Mey, and thereabouts Caithness assumes a cheerful, almost bustling mien. The scent of clover hangs in the air and the little townships are surrounded by bright green patches of fields, full in season, of hay-cocks.

Barrogill Castle is not far from the superb sands of Dunnet, and nearby Dunnet Head juts out into the Pentland Firth, a towering promentory. The views from this part of Caithness are magnificent. Twenty miles away the hills of Hoy rise up, blue, out of the sea, fronted by the great red 1000 foot cliffs of the island, and that strange phenomenon, the Old Man of Hoy, holds his lonely vigil.

On a clear day the tower of St. Magnus Cathedral in Kirkwall can be seen over Scapa Flow. On a late summer evening the Queen Mother will be able to look out on one of the finest sights in the world, the dim and shadowy Orkneys, lifting out of a northern sea in a profusion of colours in which mauve, ruby, emerald and gold are enchantingly mingled.

Ben Morven, Caithness — Looking along the Glen towards Braemore, with Ben Morven (highest mountain in Caithness). Maiden Pap and the "Scarabens" in the background.

The Castle of Mey: East Tower

Part of the main drive immediately prior to the Castle forecourt.

View of the South front of the Castle of Mey.

Castle of Mey

(by John Mowat)

The following article on Barrogill Castle was written in 1914 for the Viking Club by a well-known contributor to the John O'Groat Journal, Mr John Mowat, F.S.A. (Scot.), Glasgow:

Barrogill Castle, originally, known as the Castle of Mey, one of the ancient seats of the Earls of Caithness, is still a comfortable and commodious country residence. It was founded, if not built, by George, the fourth Earl of Caithness, who acquired the barony of Mey from the Bishop of Caithness in 1566.

In the castle there is a carving with the Caithness and Montrose arms and mottoes, with the initials 'G.S.' and 'E.G.' and the date '1566'. These arms are no doubt those of George, the 4th Earl, and Elizabeth Graham his wife, daughter of William, Earl of Montrose.

There is some uncertainty as to the exact date of its erection. In a footnote to the 'History of Caithness', J. T. Calder gives the date as 1606, but the building was probably carried out before this date, and the more likely period would be between the acquisition of the lands in 1566 and 1572, when the Earl granted a charter of the Mey land to his second son William, who became the first laird of Mey. William Sinclair, who is said to have been strangled in the dungeon of Girnigoe Castle by his elder brother, the imprisoned John, Master of Caithness, died unmarried. He was succeeded by his brother George, the Chancellor of Caithness and founder of the Mey family of Sinclairs and the later earls of Caithness. On the death of the earl in 1582, all his money was bequeathed to his youngest son, George of Mey. It is not unlikely that some of this money was used in completing, or adding to, the family residence between that date and his own death in 1616.

Addition to Structure

Sir James Sinclair of Mey, who was served heir to the title of the 12th Earl of Caithness in 1790, repaired and added to the structure. In Macfarlane's 'Geographical Collections', written in 1726, the House of Mey is mentioned as being in a dilapidated condition. In the 'Old Statistical Account of the Parish of Canisbay', written in 1793, Barrogill Castle is referred to as, 'renewing its age apace under the additions and embellishments it is daily receiving from its noble owner'.

Above the iron-studded doorway of the courtyard, there are Sinclair arms carved in the stone-work bearing the initials 'J.S.S.' and 'C.S.S.' joined by a heart and the date '1762'.

Though considerably modernised and added to during the last century, the castle still retains its distinctive 16th century features. Its jutting towers and corbelled turrets form a striking skyline; and seen from a distance, as it stands on a rising ground overlooking the Pentland Firth, the aspect is decidedly pleasing.

Traveller's Account — 1629

The earliest account of the Castle of Mey is given by William Lithgow, the traveller, who visited, and was entertained by Sir William Sinclair during the winter of 1629. He wrote and dedicated to the Earl of Caithness, a long grandiloquent description of the building and the hospitality he received from the Laird of Mey:

'Flank'd with the Marine coast, prospective stands,
Right opposite the Orcade Iles and Lands;
Where I for floures, ingorg'd strong wines of Spain,
And liquored French, both Red and White amaine;
Which Palace doth contain, two four-squared courts
Graft with brave words, where the Art-drawn pensile sports
On Hall, high Chambers, Galleries, Office Bowres
Cells, Rooms and Turrets, Platforms, Stately Towres.'

In 1876, King Edward and Queen Alexandra, as Prince and Princess of Wales, visited Barrogill Castle as guests of James, the 14th Earl, who was engineering tutor to the King and his brothers and the inventor of the 'Caithness steam carriage', the first self-propelled road vehicle. In front of the castle grows a horse-chestnut planted by the King, and an ash tree planted by the Queen.

Antique Building

In internal arrangements, as well as architectural features the castle bears evidence of antiquity. There is the vaulted kitchen with its huge fireplace and iron rings, the dungeon and similar gruesome relics of other days. It also has its traditions of blood-stained floors and haunted rooms. On the walls of the halls and principal rooms, hang many portraits of those who figured in the early history of Caithness. Here also may be seen the old coloured arms of 'Lord Sen-Klar', with the family motto, 'Commit thy work to God', found in Roslin Chapel and forwarded to the north.

In 1889, on the death of George Philip Alexander Sinclair the 15th earl of the Sinclair line the fourth and last of the Mey family the estate and ancient residence of the earldom was willed to a college friend, Mr Heathcote Sinclair.

Right: The Sinclair Arms carved in the stonework above the iron studded door in the court yard.

(Above). The Castle of Mey. Viewed from the West.

(Left): Wall lanterns adorn the entrance to the Castle. (Right): The sandstone panel above the window of the dining room on the south wall of the Castle bearing the Queen Mothers Cypher (E.R.) was carved by Hew Lorimer sculptor. Son of Sir Robert Lorimer the eminent Scottish architect.

Princess Margaret's First Visit to Caithness

Flying from Edzell, Angus, on Monday 8th August, Queen Elizabeth the Queen Mother, made a special visit to Barrogill Castle, recently purchased by her as a summer residence. She was accompanied by Princess Margaret who was paying her first visit to Caithness.

Along with the Queen Mother was her Lady-in-Waiting, Lady Jean Rankin; also in the party was Sqdn.-Leader P. Townsend, Equerry.

Few people were aware that the Royal visitors were due to arrive at Wick. It was a public holiday, otherwise the news would have spread quickly and a large number of people would have been at the Airport. The 'plane, a Viking of the Queen's Flight, landed shortly after 11. Only a handful of people were present, and, just as the 'plane touched down, a score of children from houses in the vicinity arrived on the scene.

They were delighted to see the Queen Mother and Princess Margaret who smiled and waved to them. The Queen Mother wore a black dress, black hat and silver fox fur, while Princess Margaret wore a loose fawn travelling coat.

The visitors were met by Commander C.G. Vyner and Lady Doris Vyner, at whose home, the House of the Northern Gate, the Queen Mother stayed on her two previous visits to Caithness.

This was Princess Margaret's first visit to the county and was unfortunate that she saw it under such disagreeabl conditions. The day was dull and cold and drizzling rain set i later.

The Queen and the Princess drove in Commander Vyner car to Dunnet and lunched with Commander and Lad Vyner.

In the afternoon they motored the six miles fro Commander Vyner's home to Barrogill Castle. Whi passing through Mey, a number of villagers gathered as the went to the Castle nearby.

By this time, the weather had cleared and the sun shone intervals. The visitors stayed for over an hour viewing th Castle, the grounds and the distant scenery. It is understoo that Princess Margaret was very much impressed with th Castle and surroundings.

Departure

The Royal visitors arrived at Wick Airport about 5pm This time a crowd of about 150 had gathered to see ther depart. As the Queen Mother and Princess Margaret left th car to walk to the 'plane, there were loud cheers from th children who waved enthusiastically. Both the Queen Moth and Princess Margaret smilingly acknowledged and waved i return. They were seen waving again from the windows the 'plane.

The 'plane was airborne at 5.15 and flew South to Edzel

1955: The Queen Mother, Princess Margaret and Commander and Lady Vyner at Dunnet.

OCTOBER 1952

Queen Mother in Caithness

Attends Church Service in Canisbay

During her fourth visit to Caithness — she arrived at Wick Airport on Saturday 11 October — Queen Elizabeth, the Queen Mother has enjoyed most favourable weather on the whole. Wednesday, particularly, was ideal, calm and sunny, enabling the Royal visitor to see the county at its best.

The Queen Mother flew from Edzell in a Viking of the Queen's Flight and the 'plane landed at Wick at 12.45. About 50 people, mostly children, were present and they gave Her Majesty a rousing cheer when she stepped from the plane. She acknowledged with a smile and a wave.

The Queen Mother was accompanied by her niece, the Hon. Elizabeth Elphinstone. They were met by Commander C. G. Vyner and Lady Doris Vyner, in whose car they drove to Dunnet where they were the guests of Commander and Lady Vyner at their home, the House of the Northern Gate.

Along with her host and hostess, the Royal visitor attended the mid-day service in Canisbay South Church on Sunday. She was met at the church door by Rev. Nigel Johnstone (35), a native of Edinburgh. He has been minister of Canisbay United Congregation since the Union in 1950.

The congregation worship in Canisbay Old and Canisbay South on alternate Sundays. Canisbay South Church, built in 1845 following the Disruption, overlooks the Pentland Firth. The Old Church was built in pre-Reformation days and it was there that the Earls of Caithness who, occupied Barrogill Castle, worshipped.

There was a fairly large congregation at the service which was conducted by Mr Johnstone. Praise was led by the choir and the organist was Miss Edna Sinclair, Clairlea, Gills, Canisbay. The church beadle, who was at the door when the Queen Mother arrived and departed, is 27-year-old Mr Alexander Cormack, Kirkstyle.

It is understood that during her visit, the Queen Mother made arrangements in connection with the re-decorating and furnishing of the Castle which is to be completely modernised. The former owner, Capt. F. B. Imbert-Terry, is still in residence and will vacate the premises this week-end.

Her Majesty made frequent visits to the Castle during her six-day stay in the county.

When in residence at the Castle of Mey, the Queen Mother worships at Canisbay Old Church, built in the form of a cross. Pictured here in the early 1950s.

Removal from Barrogill Castle

FORMER TENANT DEPARTS

October 1952

The former owner of Barrogill Castle, Captain F. B. Imbert-Terry, who had been in occupation for 24 years, left the premises on Monday morning the 20th of October to go to his new home, Tomich House, Beauly.

Shortly afterwards, two vans belonging to the well-known removal firm of Pickfords arrived at the castle to load Capt. Imbert-Terry's furniture for transfer to Beauly. It is expected that the removal will be completed by tomorrow (Saturday).

Supervising the removal is Mr C. Allan, who has been butler at Barrogill since 1928, and who in fact superintended the installation of the furniture when Capt. Imbert-Terry took over the castle and estate.

After Saturday, the only persons in the castle will be Mr Charles Tait (36), a native of Peterhead, his wife and two young children. Mrs Tait is a native of Mey. Mr Tait, who has been gardener at Barrogill for the past four years, is being retained in the employment of the Queen Mother.

Only necessary repairs will be carried out at the castle meantime and it will be some time yet before any major alterations and improvements are carried out. The castle is to be completely modernised and the preliminary arrangements have been settled.

Major Hugh Macdonald, architect, Thurso, is now proceeding to authorise the work.

Long Established Firm

The firm of Pickfords has branches throughout the whole of Britain, its most northerly branch being at Inverness and it has agents in Caithness. It arranges overseas removals as well.

It was established over 300 years ago, starting in 1647. The firm has many historic associations. In 1834 it transported the furniture and effects of Thomas Carlyle from the island of Arran to Chelsea, to the great satisfaction of Carlyle who was pleased at the low cost and the performance.

QUEEN MOTHER'S CHRISTMAS CARD

November 1952

While signs of the coming Coronation can be seen in the shops already displaying Christmas goods, the Royal Christmas cards however, are not likely to choose a Coronation theme — at least not that of Queen Elizabeth the Queen Mother (states a London correspondent).

It seems very likely that the picture of her card will be of her new Caithness home, the Castle of Mey. Her Majesty has collected a number of photographic views of the Castle, and from these she will probably select an aspect of the building and its setting which an artist will incorporate into her Royal greeting card.

Convict's carpet for Castle of Mey

November 1952

A beautiful carpet, priced at £100 and made by a man presently serving a prison sentence, will be presented to the Queen Mother by the Birmingham County District of the British Legion for use in her Caithness residence, the Castle of Mey.

The carpet, 13 feet by 11 feet, was the largest single exhibit on show at an exhibition of spare-time work undertaken by men in 65 prisons throughout the country, and was the only item for sale.

The manufacture of the carpet took the prisoner nearly 500 hours to complete, working through all his spare time for six months in gaol. The authorities refused to reveal the name of the man. He will not gain financially for his work as the money goes to help to defray the cost of providing teacher and materials for classes held in prisons.

Queen Mother's Privacy Will Be Respected

December 1952

Touring buses not allowed in Castle grounds

The Minister of Transport, Mr Alan Lennox-Boyd, has given Sir David Robertson, M.P., an assurance that companies who have received permission to run bus tours to the village of Mey will not be allowed to go into the Castle grounds.

In a question to the Minister on this subject, Sir David asked the number of applications for running omnibuses to the Castle of Mey which had been made between 1st April, 1931, and 31st October, 1952.

Mr Lennox-Boyd, in a written answer, stated that the Licensing Authority had informed him that only two applications could at present be traced.

One was made in October, 1951, for a group of tours from Wick and the other in September, 1952, for tours from eight places in Caithness to various destinations, including the village of Mey.

"None of the tours go to the Castle, which is about a mile from the village", he added.

No Representative

Sir David also requested the reason why the Caithness member of the Traffic Commissioners' Panel was not included among the Commissioners who recently sat in Inverness and granted eight applications for bus tours in the Castle of Mey, or any other occasions for over twelve years.

Mr Lennox-Boyd explained that he was required by the Road Traffic Act (1930) to appoint to the Licensing Authority for Scotland one member only from the panel of nominees of County Councils to attend sittings anywhere in Scotland.

No more than three or four deputies were needed to cover the members' absences. His predecessors had tried to spread the honours of office widely, but he was sorry it had not been possible so far to appoint the Caithness nominee.

Bus Tours to Castle of Mey

Traffic Chairman's Reply to Council's Protest

Caithness County Council failed to take advantage of the opportunity they had to lodge objections to the granting of a licence for bus tours to the Castle of Mey, recently bought by Queen Elizabeth the Queen Mother as a summer residence.

Making this statement in Aberdeen on Friday 21st November, following criticism by members of the County Council who objected to what they called "the invasion of the Queen Mother's privacy", Mr A. Robertson, deputy licensing authority for Scotland, said that full details of the application were included in the authority's publication (Notices and Proceedings) No. 425, which was sent to all county clerks, town clerks and chief constables in Scotland. No representations were received from the local authorities in Caithness.

The criticism of the permission for bus tours to the Castle was made by the County Council at a meeting of the Administration and Finance Committee at Wick on Thursday 20th November last week, when Brigadier G. D. K. Murray, County Convener, said he had observed from Press reports that the Traffic Commissioners, at a sitting in Inverness, had granted Scottish Omnibuses, Ltd., a licence to run those tours from eight different points.

Mr Robertson gave an assurance, when he made his statement at Aberdeen, that the authority were not forgetful of the circumstances obtaining at Mey and would attach conditions to the licence to ensure that privacy will not be disturbed.

He added however, that the authority were only concerned with public tours and had no jurisdiction over private bus parties, and much less over private cars.

With reference to the complaint that Caithness had not been represented on the bench at the hearing of this application, Mr Robertson said that was because the Ministry of Transport had not chosen a representative from Caithness for inclusion in the panel.

Following Mr Robertson's statement at Aberdeen that conditions would be attached to the licences granted to run tours to the Castle of Mey, Brig. Murray and Provost John Sinclair, Thurso, have made public statements expressing the view that the County Council would need to know more about the restrictions to be imposed.

"You can control the buses, but you cannot control the people when they arrive", Brig. Murray told a reporter.

"It is quite true", he added, "that we do get copies of the publication giving the applications which are to come before the Traffic Commissioners, but the Authority might have, in the circumstances, written asking for our opinion".

He said that since 1939, he had been nominated by Caithness County Council as their representative to the traffic licensing panel, but as yet he had not been chosen.

Provost Sinclair's View

"We do not want the same position as exists at Balmoral when the Royal Family are in residence, especially on a Sunday", declared Provost Sinclair.

Although he agreed that the same number of people would not go to Mey Castle as did to Balmoral, Provost Sinclair said that members of the Council did not like the idea at all, of sightseers arriving in buses and gazing at the Queen Mother and the Castle.

"We are all interested in Royalty, and we are proud and pleased that the Queen Mother should reside in the county, but we do not like the idea of her being 'mobbed' whenever she appears", said Provost Sinclair.

He did not think that Caithness people would do that. They had seen her in town and in the county and they had respected her wishes for privacy.

"We should like her to enjoy the quietness of our countryside," he commented.

Queen Elizabeth the Queen Mother with Commander and Lady Vyner in the grounds of The Castle of Mey.

The Queen Mother, who is a keen salmon fisher, was out on Saturday the 7th of August for five hours on the Thurso river, one of the best known salmon rivers in Scotland.

It was an ideal day for an outing if not for fishing. She was accompanied by Commander Vyner and Lady Doris Vyner, Lady Delia Peel, Lady-in-Waiting, and Sir Arthur Penn, Private Secretary.

Two noted local expert anglers were with the party. They were Mr David Sinclair (52), river superintendent, Halkirk, who was with the Queen Mother; and Mr Donald Murray (65), 6 Castle Street, Thurso (a native of Wick), who was with Commander Vyner and Sir Arthur Penn, the only others in the party who were fishing.

In an interview with the *John O'Groat Journal*, Mr Murray said: "We saw plenty of fish on the move but none was taking. The day was calm and thundery and Her Majesty appreciated that the conditions were not favourable for fishing.

"The Queen Mother throws a beautiful line. She is a keen angler and fished four hours continuously, enjoying every minute of it."

The party were out from 11.30 to 5.30. First they fished on No. 4 beat at Hoy and later at No. 12 beat at Dirlot.

They lunched at the river amid the beautiful surroundings of Dirlot which Her Majesty much admired. She was specially interested in the ruins of the old castle there and the ancient cemetery.

Her Majesty attended the noon service in Canisbay Ol Church on Sunday. This was the first time that sh worshipped in the Old Church; on her former visits to th county she attended Dunnet Church and Canisbay Ne Church.

Wearing a grey ensemble with hat to match and carrying silver fox fur, the Royal visitor was accompanied b Commander Vyner and Lady Doris Vyner, Lady Delia Pee Lady-in-Waiting, Sir Arthur Penn and Mr Henry Vyne son of Commander and Lady Doris Vyner.

There was a large congregation, including a number c visitors home from the South and overseas. The Quee Mother was met at the church door by Rev. Nigel Johnstone minister of the united congregation in Canisbay, and wh had conducted the service in Canisbay New Church whe Her Majesty was in Caithness last October.

It was a warm, calm day with hardly a ripple in th Pentland Firth. A number of visitors were outside the churc when the Queen Mother arrived and she turned to smile t them as she entered the church.

Canisbay Old Church is a pre-Reformation building standing on the site of the first Canisbay Church built in th 12th century. It is 3½ miles from the Castle of Mey and wa the family worshipping place of the Earls of Caithness whe they occupied the Castle.

Her Majesty arrives at Wick Airport from Prestwick.

The Royal visitor at Wick Airport before departing for London. She is chatting to Air Commodore Sir Edward Fielden, Air Officer commanding The Queen's Flight. Lady Hyde, Lady-in-Waiting, is seen on the left with Commander C.G. Vyner. During her weekend in the county, the Queen Mother spent most of her time at the Castle of Mey making further plans for the alterations and repairs which are proceeding there before she takes up residence.

Queen Mother's First Public Engagement in Caithness.

Queen Elizabeth the Queen Mother, while on a week's visit to Caithness, attended her first public function in the county when she presented prizes to farmers at a ceremony held at Achalone Farm, Halkirk. The prizes were won in a competition, organised by the North of Scotland College of Agriculture, to encourage land reclamation in the county. As a special prize, Mr Maitland Mackie, chairman of the College governors, donated a trophy to be known as the Mackie Cup.

It is an incentive to small farmers and the first person to win the trophy was Mr Alexander Budge, Achalone, who has 50 acres of arable ground, 20 of which have been reclaimed from heather.

Two other farmers were awarded diplomas for second and third places. They were Mr G.M.B. Henderson, Scrabste and Mr Kenneth Mackenzie, Achagie.

The fourth place, for which there was no prize, went to M Donald Gulloch, Lower Stemster, John O'Groats.

Brigadier G.D.K. Murray, Vice-Lieutenant of Caithness a governor of the College and a leading farmer in the North presided at the ceremony which was attended by over 6 persons including competitors and their wives.

In a speech after the presentation of the prizes, the Quee Mother said: "I am very glad that my first public engagemen in this county — for which, as I am beginning to know it, feel an increasing affection — should be for a purpose of suc outstanding importance to-day: the better cultivation of th land."

Her Majesty arriving at Achalone, where she was welcomed by Brig. G.D.K. Murray, Vice-Lieutenant of Caithness (right), an Mrs Murray (centre).

Eleven-year-old Kathleen Budge, youngest daughter of Mr and Mrs Alexr. Budge, Achalone, presenting a bouquet to the Queen Mother before the start of the ceremony in the marquee. Others in the picture (left to right) — Mrs Murray, Sir Arthur Penn (Her Majesty's financial secretary), Brig. Murray, Mr Maitland Mackie, Principal M.A.H. Tincker, Mr J.W. Grant and Mr T. Graham (all of the North of Scotland College of Agriculture).

The Queen Mother speaking to Mr Alexander Budge, Achalone, who won the premier prize in the competition.

Brig. G.D.K. Murray, Vice-Lieutenant of Caithness, addressing the company in the marquee.

Her Majesty smiles to the gathering after receiving the bouquet.

Royal Inauguration of Caithness Water Scheme

Queen Mother Performs Ceremony at Hoy

The inauguration of their regional water scheme — the rst phase of which cost £750,000 — by Queen Elizabeth the ueen Mother, on Saturday 30th April, crowned a historic :hievement for Caithness County Council. No other :heme of its kind exists in Britain. It provides water for a hole county and the method used to pump the water to e reservoirs is water power.

The ceremony took place at Hoy Pumping Station before 300 guests and many hundreds of spectators who came from all parts of the county. In performing the ceremony, Her Majesty delighted the gathering when she said that she was glad that many of her neighbours would have the same facilities from the scheme as she would have at the Castle of Mey.

A general view of the scene after the inauguration. Behind Thurso Town Band (left) one of the miniature fountains is in play. Her Majesty in happy mood, is seen speaking to Brig. Murray. On the left the sheriff principal, F.C. Watt and Mrs Murray.

n her speech during the ceremony the Queen Mother said: I am very glad to inaugurate to-day a service which will, I ope, be invaluable to the people of this county. Before the var barely one-fifth of those who live here had a supply of unning water and it is a great happiness to me to realise that n advantage which I can now myself enjoy at the Castle of Aey should also be available to a great number of my eighbours.

"This great water scheme must be a real boon and benefit o the people of Caithness. I learned that 150 miles of water nains and over 1500 individual connections have already een made and that extensions are being rapidly promoted or those whose turn has yet to come. There can be few amenities more welcome throughout the county, and it is indeed a pleasure to me to associate myself with it.

"I am glad to see that the pumping station, unlike some of its kind, has an appearance which is both workmanlike and unostentatious and is in keeping with the fair surroundings in which I constantly rejoice. I should like to offer my warm congratulations to all who have been concerned in this great endeavour.

"It now gives me much pleasure to inaugurate the regional water scheme for the county."

The Queen Mother pressed a button on the table and set the water flowing. Thereupon four small fountains in front of the station began to play.

In the main hall of the pumping station. Mr Jollans is seen explaining part of the equipment. Brig. Murray on the right, with Jame. Robertson, County clerk, on the left of the picture.

Councillor Miss L. M. Kennedy presents a silver inkstand to Her Majesty on the occasion of the inauguration of the regiona water scheme.

Queen Mother and Princess Margaret on Holiday

Queen Elizabeth the Queen Mother and Princess Margaret arrived in the North on Saturday 6th August, for a short holiday in Caithness. The Princess travelled south again on Wednesday and the Queen Mother is expected to leave to-morrow (Saturday 13th).

The Royal visitors flew from London to Inverness in a Viking of the Queen's Flight and travelled north by special train to Georgemas, where they were met by their host and hostess, Commander C.G. Vyner and Lady Doris Vyner, Dunnet, who were accompanied by their son, Mr Henry Vyner.

The train arrived shortly before seven o'clock on Saturday night and, although the weather was cold and misty with drizzling rain at times, a fairly large crowd had gathered outside the station platform to welcome the visitors.

The Queen Mother was wearing a lavender coat with hat to match and furs, while Princess Margaret wore a fawn coat and small white hat. She was carrying a camera.

Before leaving the platform, the Queen Mother spoke to Mr James Gunn, stationmaster, who has been in the railway service for 40 years, including 12 at Georgemas. Her Majesty told Mr Gunn that she had enjoyed her journey north.

The Royal visitors, who were accompanied by the Hon. Mrs Mulholland, Lady-in-Waiting, and Major Roger Seymore, Equerry, completed their journey to Dunnet by road.

During their holiday the Queen Mother and Princess Margaret, along with their host and hostess and Mr Vyner, visited the Castle of Mey almost every day.

The weather on the whole was fine and on Monday afternoon the Royal visitors took the opportunity of the warm sunny day to picnic along the coast.

Princess Margaret flies South by helicopter

Farewell: The Queen Mother bids farewell to Princess Margaret.

The Queen Mother is seen speaking to Mrs Taylor, wife of Dr William Taylor, Dunnet. Lady Doris Vyner is on the right.

Helicopter departure — a reminder of experiences during the snowstorms

A large crowd of people, including many visitors, gathered on the roadside at Dunnet early on Wednesday afternoon the 10th August, to watch the departure of Princess Margaret who flew south in a helicopter of the Queen's Flight.

The helicopter landed in a field adjoining the house of Dr Wm. Taylor, medical officer for the parish. This field was used by naval helicopters during the "Snowdrop Operations" in the severe storms last winter when Dr Taylor had to be transported to visit urgent cases which could not be reached by road.

Earlier in the day Princess Margaret, assisted by Commander C.G. Vyner, had marked the field for the landing of the helicopter.

The Queen Mother, along with her host and hostess, was at the field to bid goodbye to the Princess who wa accompanied by Major Roger Seymour, Equerry.

The helicopter, piloted by Flight-Lieut. Alan J. Lee, fle to Inverness where Princess Margaret boarded a Viking the Queen's Flight to complete her journey to Stranra where she joined the Queen and the Duke of Edinburgh o the Royal yacht Britannia.

After the Princess's departure, the Queen Mother, befo returning to the House of the Northern Gate, spoke for a fe minutes to Dr Taylor and Mrs Taylor and said that th helicopter would remind them of their experiences durin the snowstorms.

Princess Margaret came North on Saturday with Quee Elizabeth the Queen Mother for a short holiday and staye at the House of the Northern Gate, as the guest Commander Vyner and Lady Doris Vyner.

The Queen's first visit to Caithness

The Queen smiles to the crowd as she leaves the pier accompanied by the Queen Mother, Princess Anne, Prince Charles, Princess Margaret and the Princess Royal.

Her Majesty the Queen visited Caithness for the first time on Friday 12th August. She was accompanied by the Duke of Edinburgh, Prince Charles, Princess Anne, Princess Margaret and other members of the Royal party who were on their way to Aberdeen in the Royal yacht Britannia.

This was an informal three-hour stop on the journey for the special purpose of visiting Queen Elizabeth the Queen Mother at the Castle of Mey.

Nevertheless, it afforded an opportunity to the people of Caithness to give Her Majesty and the Royal Family an enthusiastic welcome to the North. It was a thrilling day for all those who were able to get to the points on the route along which Her Majesty passed.

The Queen saw Caithness for the first time in the full glory of a beautiful summer's day.

As this was not an official visit, the public were not aware which part of the coast the Royal visitors were to land. However, many hundreds of people gathered on the main road at Dunnet along which the Queen and party would pass on the way to the Castle of Mey.

The Britannia, escorted by H.M.S. destroyer, Orwell, arrived in Dunnet Bay about 3.30 in the afternoon. The yacht came close in and anchored near Dwarick Head, above which stands the House of the Northern Gate, the home of Commander C. G. Vyner and Lady Doris Vyner, with whom the Queen Mother was staying during her holiday in Caithness last week.

A fairly large crowd of people who had made the right guess, were assembled on the hillside above the shore at Dwarick Pier.

The Queen Mother was at the pier awaiting the arrival of the Queen and party. She was accompanied by the Princess Royal who had motored from Suisgill where she was on holiday; Commander C.G. Vyner, Lady Doris Vyner and their son, Mr Henry Vyner. The Hon. Mrs Mulholland, Lady-in-Waiting, and Major Roger Seymour, Equerry, were in attendance.

A small motor launch left the Britannia shortly after four o'clock and made for the pier. The Queen Mother, who had been viewing the yacht with binoculars, watched the launch's progress towards the shore and she waved from time to time.

The Queen must have been impressed by her first sight of Caithness, for Dunnet Bay, with its majestic sweep of sandy beach glimmering in the hot sun, is one of the most beautiful places in the North.

First on to the pier from the launch was Princess Anne and immediately she saw the Queen Mother she raced up the slipway towards her, to the great delight of the crowd. Loud cheers broke out from the spectators as Her Majesty stepped on to the pier and walked forward to be welcomed by the Queen Mother.

The Queen was wearing a fawn coat and head scarf. She carried a camera. Princess Margaret also wore a fawn coat and head scarf.

Among the Royal party were Princess Andrew of Greece and Prince Michael of Kent.

On the way to the waiting motor cars, the Queen smiled and waved in response to the cheering crowd.

The motor launch arrives at Dwarick Pier. The Queen Mother is seen greeting Princess Anne. On the right is the Princess Roya

Her Majesty surveys the scene as she stands on the pier.

"Haste Ye Back"

By the time the Royal cars had reached the main road at Dunnet, the crowds there had grown bigger and there were hundreds of vehicles parked in various places. Her Majesty passed through the cheering spectators, many of them visitors to Caithness and natives of the county on holiday.

There was a tea party in the Castle, following which the visitors went down to the beach below the Castle, where the Royal children had a happy time.

The Britannia had gone round to Scrabster Roads and anchored there. Alongside was H.M.S. Orwell. The yacht made a beautiful picture in the bay, standing close in to Scrabster.

Her Majesty left from Scrabster at 7p.m.; the party motoring from the Castle of Mey to the pier. Hours before the departure time crowds had taken up positions on the quays. The streets of Thurso were also thronged and, many points along the route between Mey and Thurso, people assembled to cheer Her Majesty.

The sun was still shining brightly and Thurso Bay never looked more entrancing. In the background stood Dunnet Head and Dwarick Head and the white house on top could be clearly seen.

Vessels in the harbour were gaily beflagged for the occasion. Prolonged cheering was heard along the quays as the Royal cars proceeded to the departure point.

On arriving at the departure point Her Majesty was greeted by Brig. G.D.K. Murray, Vice-Lieutenant of Caithness, who was accompanied by Mrs Murray. Also present were Provost John Sinclair, Thurso and Provost Miss B. Leith, Wick who were presented to Her Majesty.

The Royal visitors stood chatting in small groups for a few minutes before going aboard the Royal barge which was moored alongside the Thurso fishing boat Primula (Skipper Angus Mackintosh, coxswain of Thurso lifeboat). The gangway from the pier was laid over Primula's deck. The vessel flew the signal "Haste Ye Back".

Before boarding the barge, the Duke of Edinburgh stood speaking for a few minutes with Coastguard District Officer S. Harbottle and Coastguard R. McBay who were in attendance at the top of the gangway.

The scene on the quay at Scrabster when the Royal Family arrived. On the left of the picture is district officer S. Harbottle, Wick Coastguard.

The Departure from Scrabster Harbour

Excited crowds throng the quay

Princess Margaret, followed by Prince Charles and Princess Anne, Princess Andrew and Prince Michael, was first aboard the barge. Then the Duke of Edinburgh preceded the Queen down the gangway. Her Majesty stood for a moment smiling to the crowd before going aboard.

As the vessel proceeded out of the harbour, there was more loud spontaneous cheering from the crowd. The Queen Mother and her party walked to the end of the pier to watch the Royal family's departure.

Eight small yachts of the Pentland Firth Yacht Club escorted the Royal barge to the Britannia.

Hundreds of cars made for the Mey and John O'Groats area with people to watch the Britannia's passage through the Pentland Firth at 10.15. It was a beautiful evening and despite a slight haze, the view of the Firth was most impressive. Shortly after 10 o'clock, the Britannia could be seen round Dunnet Head with her escort.

The Castle of Mey was brilliantly floodlit for the occasion, as were the Britannia and her escort, as they slowly passed the Queen Mother's home.

Ground flares were lit along the foot of the castle wall and rockets and parachute flares were fired from the Castle.

As they steamed along past the Castle, the Britannia an the Orwell sent up rockets in answer. A message was flashe in morse from the Britannia and was replied to from th Castle. Still firing rockets at intervals, the Britannia o passing Mey, circled once in the Firth before proceeding o her way.

The Queen Mother and a party, including her host an hostess, stood at the rear of the Castle watching the yacht passage through the Firth.

Directing the launch into the pier at Dunnet were tw local men — Mr James Calder, Lochside, Dunnet and M James Henderson, postmaster, Dunnet.

Princess Anne was five on Monday and the event wa celebrated with a birthday tea party at Balmoral.

All the arrangements in connection with the visit were we organised by the police who gave the public every possibl scope to see as much as possible.

As Lady Doris Vyner curtseys to the Queen, the Queen Mother says goodbye to Prince Charles.

The Queen Mother watching the party going aboard the Royal Barge. On the extreme left is the Princess Royal. Others in the picture are (left to right) Mrs Murray; Provost Bessie Leith, Wick; Provost John Sinclair, Thurso and Brig. G.D.K. Murray, Vice-Lieutenant of Caithness.

The Royal Barge heads out of Scrabster Harbour to the Royal Yacht Britannia.

"We lost our hearts to it"

Her Majesty saw the Castle of Mey in the splendour of a summer day and saw it again floodlit at night and she and the other members of the family lost their hearts to it.

As the Royal yacht passed the Castle on its way along the north coast to Aberdeen, the Queen sent the following message to the Queen Mother:

"Castle of Mey looks terribly impressive and we are sorry to depart. We have lost our hearts to it from the start. We have had a glorious day."

The Queen Mother's reply was: "We have all been very happy to have you with us. Please come again soon."

Queen Mother Thanks Wick Coastguards

District Officer Sam Harbottle, Wick Coastguard Station, who, along with other members of the staff, was responsible for the pyrotechnic display at the Castle and also for providing a signaller to reply to the message flashed from the Royal yacht Britannia, has received the following letter from Major Roger Seymour, Equerry to Queen Elizabeth the Queen Mother:—

"I am commanded by Queen Elizabeth the Queen Moth to write and express Her Majesty's very grateful thanks yourself and to your men, for all the assistance which yo provided on the occasion of the Queen's visit to Caithnes

"Queen Elizabeth felt that the floodlighting of the Cast and the display of rockets were the greatest possible succe and that it was largely thanks to the efforts of yourself a your men that this was so.

"Her Majesty also very much appreciated your thought bringing a signaller to the Castle, by means of whom H Majesty was able to exchange messages with the Britanni

"Queen Elizabeth feels that last Friday was indeed a gre day for Caithness and knows that you must be very happy having played such a considerable part to ensure its success

"Once again, I am to express Her Majesty's gratitude to of you for the very excellent work that you did."

Mr Robert Finlayson, electrical engineer, Wick, w responsible for the floodlighting of the Castle.

A beautiful view of the floodlit Castle, seen from the seaward side.

First pictures of the Queen Mother at the Castle of Mey

The Queen Mother pictured in the grounds of the Castle with her favourite corgi, Honey.

The delightful drawing room at the Castle of Mey.

The staircase leading out of the main hall.

A view from the top of the staircase.

The Pink Bedroom.

Her Majesty is standing beside the artistic gateway at the rear of the Castle. In the background, the Orkney Islands can be see across the Firth.

The Queen Mother examining flowers in the beautiful gardens.

The Queen Mother's Corgi, Honey, appears to have other ideas in this charming photograph of Her Majesty in the forecourt of the Castle.

Her Majesty in the gardens of the Castle of Mey.

Her Majesty pictured beside the cannon in the grounds of the Castle of Mey.

The Queen Mother pictured by the Wicket gate at the rear of the Castle.

The Royal Standard flying from the Castle of Mey.

The Queen Mother's Rug: Two leading members of the WRI movement present a beautiful hand made rug to the Queen Mother at the Castle of Mey. Over 600 members in the Caithness branches helped to stitch the rug.

JUNE 1956

Queen Mother's Holiday in Caithness

At Wick Airport. — Her Majesty is seen with Lady Doris Vyner and Commander C.G. Vyner on her left. On her right is Brig. G.D.K. Murray, Vice-Lieutenant of Caithness.

Queen Elizabeth the Queen Mother returns to London today (Friday) 15 June, after a week's holiday in Caithness. She arrived the previous Saturday and has been staying at the Castle of Mey, her new Scottish home.

Her Majesty, who flew from London in a Viking of the Queen's Flight, was officially welcomed at Wick Airport by Brigadier G.D.K. Murray, Vice-Lieutenant of the county, to whom she said: "I am delighted to be back in Caithness."

Commander C.G. Vyner and Lady Doris Vyner, at whose home in Dunnet the Queen Mother stayed on former visits to the county, were also present to greet her.

Mr Geoffrey T. Stanley, airport commandant of the Northern Group, and Mr T. Somerville, airport manager, were in attendance, as also was Mr John W. Georgeson, chief constable of Caithness.

The 'plane touched down about 3.20 p.m. The day was warm and sunny and a fairly large crowd, including visitors, had gathered to see the Queen Mother's arrival.

Her Majesty was accompanied by Lady Fermoy, Lady-in-Waiting, and Sir Arthur Penn, her financial secretary.

The Royal visitor left for the Castle of Mey by car, and travelling with her were Lady Doris Vyner and Lady Fermoy.

The warm weather continued throughout the week-end, but unfortunately broke on Tuesday, when there was heavy rain, and it has remained cool since.

At Canisbay Church

On Sunday, the Queen Mother attended the noon service in Canisbay New Church. The service was conducted by the minister, Rev. Nigel Johnstone. Her Majesty was interested to meet the recently appointed beadle, Mrs Elizabeth Banks, New Houses, Canisbay, the only woman beadle in Caithness.

On leaving the church, the Queen Mother spoke to Mrs Banks and asked her if she liked her work.

Among the congregation were five Wick Girl Guides, all members of the 1st St. Fergus Company. They were camping for the weekend at Freswick and attended the service in uniform.

The Royal visitor noticed the Guides and stopped for a few minutes to speak to Anne Dunnet (13), 16 Tolbooth Lane. She inquired from Anne about Guiding in Caithness and asked her to which Company she and her friends belong. The other Guides were Catherine Allan, Betty Campbell, Jean Begg and Linda Egerton.

Despite the break in the weather, the Royal visitor was out and about shopping on some occasions and for motor runs on others.

Children strawberry picking in the Castle of Mey gardens. — By kind permission of course!

Castle of Mey gardens were open to the public for the first time by kind permission of Queen Elizabeth the Queen Mother. Th occasion was in aid of Scotland's Gardens Scheme. Despite unfavourable weather, large crowds of people from all parts o Caithness and beyond, flocked to Mey. Some of the visitors are seen going round the gardens.

Queen Mother in Residence at Mey
Public Engagements in the North

Freedom Ceremony at Wick Saturday, August 11.

Queen Elizabeth the Queen Mother is in residence at the Castle of Mey. She arrived on Tuesday, 7th August, having flown from London in a Viking of the Queen's Flight. She has two public engagements in the county.

The first will take place to-morrow (Saturday 11th August) when she will receive the Freedom of the Royal Burgh of Wick. The ceremony will be held at the Riverside. A week later, she will travel to Thurso to name Thurso's new lifeboat, the Dunnet Head, which function will be held at Scrabster Harbour. On Wednesday 8th August this week, Her Majesty flew to Orkney by helicopter to open Kirkwall's new playing field.

At Wick Airport

When she arrived at Wick, shortly after 3 p.m., the Queen Mother was welcomed at the airport by Viscount Thurso, Lord Lieutenant of Caithness, who was accompanied by Viscountess Thurso.

Others in attendance were Miss B. Leith, Provost, Col. J.J. Robertson, and Major James B. Simpson, Deputy Lieutenants, the Hon. Robin M. Sinclair and the Hon. Mrs Sinclair, Mr G.T. Stanley, airport commandant for the Northern Group, and Mr T. Somerville, airport manager.

Her Majesty, who wore a light blue coat with hat to match, was accompanied by Lady Hyde, Lady-in-Waiting, and the Master of Sinclair, Equerry.

The day was dull and blustery, but at times there were bursts of sunshine. Quite a crowd of people, including visitors, had gathered at the airport to see the Royal visitor's arrival.

Later, the Queen Mother left by car for the Castle of Mey.

Put Out Your Flags

By mid-week, a start had already been made by shopkeepers and householders to decorate their premises, and the town presents a bright and gay appearance. Much more can still be done to add to the gaiety and the Town Council hope that as many as possible will respond to their appeal to put out flags and bunting.

After being welcomed by Viscount Thurso, Lord Lieutenant, at Wick Airport, the Queen Mother is greeted by Viscountess Thurso.

Helicopter flight

The Royal visitor received an ovation when she opened the King George V Playing Field in the afternoon.

In her speech, the Queen Mother said that whenever she went to Caithness and looked from her drawing-room window, her gaze was ever drawn northwards to Orkney. Sometimes the islands lay shrouded in mist and cloud. Then the sun appeared, the Pentland Firth sparkled and gleamed, and the islands shone like jewels in their lovely setting.

"I always look at the islands with pleasure", the Queen Mother said, "and it is a great happiness to set foot upon the land which has beckoned me so often." There were now more than 100 King George Playing Fields in the United Kingdom and Northern Ireland, and Kirkwall's was one of 86 memorial fields in Scotland.

The Queen Mother said: "Each year our cities are increasing in size, and the impact of the wireless, the cinema, and television, all admirable in their way, tend to create a way of life in which our children are spectators rather than participants at games and sports.

"There is a danger that this may produce a generation of lookers-on who lack the initiative, self-reliance and enterprise of our ancestors."

The Queen Mother spoke in a half-gale and at times her voice could scarcely be heard over the loudspeakers.

Before the opening ceremony, the Queen Mother i spected a guard of honour provided by 430 Coast Regimer Royal Artillery (T.A.), and afterwards she drove throu the beflagged streets of Kirkwall with Provost James Flet

The Queen Mother wore a powder blue costume with h and coat to match, and carried a grey fox fur. She w greeted by Mr P.N. Sutherland Graeme, Lord Lieutenant Orkney, to whom she said that she had seen Orkney ofte from the air and from the Castle of Mey and it was ver pleasant to be there.

The biggest crowds ever assembled in Kirkwall saw th Queen Mother drive up to the kirk green, in front of S Magnus Cathedral, where she was received by Provost Flet The provost presented Lord Clydesmuir, chairman of th National Playing Fields Association (Scotland), the burg magistrates, and town councillors.

The Queen Mother was shown round the Cathedral b Provost Flett, who told her something of its proud histo and its associations with the Norse era. Kirkwall Tow Council were hosts at lunch in a local hotel.

Before her next engagement, the opening of the ne playing field, the Queen Mother was presented with a straw backed Orkney chair as a memento of the visit.

Her Majesty flew by helicopter to Orkney to perform a public engagement in Kirkwall. A helicopter from the Royal Naval Station Lossiemouth, arrived earlier in the day and came down in a field about 100 yards in front of the Castle.

Freedom Ceremony in the Royal Burgh

Cheering Crowds Greet Wick's Youngest Burgess

When she was presented with the Freedom of Wick on aturday, 11th August — the first woman ever to receive it – Queen Elizabeth the Queen Mother described the honour s "a symbol of the kindness which I have always found waiting me in Caithness".

Expressing her delight at having a home in Caithness, Her Majesty said: "When I came here I felt at home and among iends."

As is well known, Caithness captivated the Queen Mother when she first visited it in 1952 and this she made clear in her eply after receiving the Burgess ticket.

Certainly, the county was not looking its best on Saturday – it rained incessantly throughout the proceedings — but ne unfortunate weather failed to rob the Burgh's most nemorable day of its impressiveness, dignity and pageantry.

The gracious qualities of Wick's youngest Burgess were never more apparent and more appreciated by the people of Caithness than on this grey, rainy day when, from the first moment of her arrival until her departure five hours later, he radiated that charm which endears her to all.

Her Majesty has another public engagement to-morrow Saturday 18th August) when she will visit Thurso to name the new lifeboat, the Dunnet Head. The ceremony takes place at 3 p.m. The Queen Mother, who is in residence at the Castle of Mey, will leave on Tuesday after being a fortnight n the county.

Wick's Welcome

The Queen Mother motored from the Castle of Mey and rrived in the town at 11.15. Even in the rain, the streets ooked gay with flags, bunting and decorations. Crowds hronged High Street and Bridge Street, which were closed o traffic.

At the Town Hall, where the largest number of people were gathered, Viscount Thurso, Lord Lieutenant of the County, and Miss Bessie Leith, Provost, awaited the arrival f the Royal visitor.

At 11.15, a rousing cheer rang through Bridge Street as Her Majesty's car approached. She was accompanied by ady Hyde, Lady-in-Waiting, and the Master of Sinclair, querry.

The Queen Mother wore a lavender coat and dress with oral hat to match. She carried a platina fox stole. Her jewellery consisted of a pearl necklace and a diamond lapel ornament.

On entering the Hall, the Royal visitor was presented with a bouquet of roses and carnations by little Christine Begg, daughter of Mr. A.S. Begg, burgh surveyor.

Inside the Hall, the Magistrates and other members of the Council, officials and others were presented. The Queen Mother also signed the distinguished visitors' book.

At The Riverside

It was raining steadily when the Queen Mother proceeded to the Riverside where a huge crowd had gathered. Her Majesty first inspected a Guard of Honour of the Seaforth Highlanders, Fort George, who then gave a Royal Salute. Commanding the guard was Captain J.C.O.R. Hopkinson.

The Guard of Honour; comprising 48 N.C.O.'s and men, arrived from Fort George the previous day under the command of Major K.L.F. Forshaw-Wilson, second-in-command of Fort George depot.

Among the guard were five young Caithness National Servicemen, two of whom belong to Wick. They are L/Cpl. Robert Flett and Pte. Arthur Robertson, both Wick; Pte. Alexander Sutherland, Watten; Pte. David Begg, Dunbeath, and Pte. Donald Munro, Thurso.

When the Queen Mother took her place on the platform, which was covered with a wide canopy, she received a great cheer from the assembly and acknowledged with a wave of her hand.

Platform Party

Along with Her Majesty and the Provost on the platform were: — Lord and Lady Thurso; Bailies W.S. Finlayson, G. Gunn and J.G.Macleod; Dean of Guild G. Sinclair, Mr D.S. Davidson (town clerk) and Rev. W.N. Scott. Commander C.G. Vyner and Lady Doris Vyner; Lady Hyde and the Master of Sinclair; Sheriff-Principal F.C. Watt; Brig. G.D.K. Murray, Convener of Caithness, and Provost J. Sinclair, Thurso.

The proceedings commenced with the singing of the 23rd Psalm, led by the Salvation Army Band, under Bandmaster Wm. McKain. Rev. W.N. Scott, Old Parish Church, then offered prayer.

On her arrival at the Town Hall, where she was met by Viscount Thurso and Miss Bessie Leith, Provost (above), the Royal visitc was presented with a bouquet by five-year-old Christine Begg (below). On the right is Major K.L.F. Forshaw-Wilson, who was i charge of the guard of honour of the Seaforth Highlanders.

Rainswept Bridge Street, Wick, thronged with excited townspeople, as the Queen Mother arrives at the Town Hall.

A wee dog entertains the crowd at the Riverside, Wick, as they await the arrival of the Queen Mother.

(Overleaf) August 1956. Her Majesty Queen Elizabeth the Queen Mother inspects the Guard of Honour at the Riverside.

Welcoming the Royal visitor, Provost Leith said they were greatly honoured and rejoiced exceedingly in the presence of Her Majesty. "This is a great day for the citizens of the Royal Burgh of Wick and their many friends and relations scattered throughout our own country and the world," she said. "A multitude not with us here, will be with us in spirit."

The Royal Family

Continuing, the Provost paid a well-deserved tribute to the Queen Mother. She said: "The Royal Family is the centre of our national life and Your Majesty has played a great part in cementing the bonds of unity and friendship which exist between the crown and the people, not only of our own land but in the commonwealth of nations and, indeed, throughout the world. You have taken a leading part in the hopes and inspirations, prosperity and advancement of our peoples. Not only so, but in periods of crisis and peril, Your Majesty has set a noble example of courage and steadfastness. We are proud of Your Majesty's Scottish descent and your inheritance of that independence which has always been a distinguishing characteristic of our national life. But when one has described all the evident bonds between Your Majesty and the people, there is still an indefinable something which knits us all together."

Recalling that Wick had been a Royal Burgh since 1589 when King James VI had granted the Charter, which was still in the town's possession and much treasured, the Provost said the King's chief aim in doing so was to give security of life and presence to the people of Wick during those troublesome times, and his aim had been successful. Three years earlier Wick had been burned by invaders from Sutherland, and only the impregnable walls of Girnigoe Castle had turned them back. It was this disaster which inspired the Earl of Caithness to appeal for a Royal Charter, for even in those days, an attack on a Royal Burgh would not go unavenged by the State. The Charter expressed the hope that Wick would have a civilising effect on the surrounding district, a task which, it was hoped had been nobly performed.

Historic Links

"It is a link with today's historic event," she said, "that it was the same Earl of Caithness who was the main builder of the Castle of Mey, which building was started by his grandfather.

"For some obscure reason, the Earl who granted the Charter was usually referred to as 'the wicked Earl'. All that this seemed to mean was that he was a man of infinite resource. The so-called wicked Earl was a misunderstood man, a personality in advance of his time.

"There was a shortage of currency at that period — what we would now call a credit squeeze," she continued. "The Earl met this by installing a noted coiner, by the name of Arthur Smith, in one of the nooks of Girnigoe Castle, but this piece of enlightened counter-disinflation was met then, as it would be now, by the appropriate intervention of the law! Whatever may be the rights of the story, the builder of the Castle of Mey and the man who secured our Charter ought to be in our memory today."

Another historical connection with the ceremony came from the story of St. Fergus. St. Fergus was a bishop who lived in the eighth century. He came to Wick from Strathearn where he had founded three churches. He evangelised Wick so well that he became its patron saint and his figure was perpetuated in the Burgh Coat of Arms. After leaving Wick, he made his pilgrimage to Buchan and thence to Glamis, where he founded a church. It was in Glamis that he died and was buried. Both Glamis and Wick had an annual fair called Fergusmas after St. Fergus. In Wick, this fair lasted well into the 19th century.

"The association which Your Majesty has formed with Caithness and the Burgh of Wick by taking up residence the venerable Castle of Mey," continued the Provost, "h greatly quickened the deep affection and abiding loyal which we, far removed as we are from the centre of thing have always felt for the Royal Family."

After recalling happy incidents which took place shor after the Queen Mother's first visit to the coun particularly the opportunity given to school pupils to see t Royal visitor, the Provost quoted the following poem whi she considered appropriate to this great occasion:

"CAITHNESS MAKES HER CURTSEY"

We're proud today,
For the beloved Queen Mother comes here to stay,
Not alone a Royal smile passing this way —
But coming to rest in her Castle of Mey.

So there shall be
A hundred thousand welcomes o'er land and sea,
The greeting of the Celts, its ancient heraldry,
For a Queen who has served right loyally.

Lest any dare,
To say this land is bleak or bare —
Pray have a care, yea have a care,
For the eyes of a Queen have rested there —
And behold the land is forever fair.

"The freedom of a Royal Burgh," said the Provost, " regarded as the highest personal honour which can conferred by the citizens on those who in internation national or domestic affairs, have earned the gratitude of t entire community, and this Your Majesty has done in f measure. May I be permitted at this point to say that we ha on our Burgess Roll the name of His Royal Highness Prin Albert, Duke of Edinburgh, who received the freedom Wick in 1882. The Duke of Edinburgh is a name with whi Your Majesty is no doubt familiar.

"This day we feel so proud to have the illustrious name Your Majesty on our Burgess Roll — the very first lady a the very first Royal lady whose name will adorn it. T privilege of presiding on an occasion like this is usually man's one but, as a woman Provost of this ancient and Roy Burgh, I have the very great honour to express to yo Majesty the joy, happiness and affection of all our citizens. is my humble duty and that of the Magistrates, Councillc and townspeople to tender for Your Majesty's gracio acceptance the Freedom of the Royal Burgh of Wick."

Gifts Presented

Concluding, the Provost said: "It is my great honour present to you this Burgess ticket. To mark this gre occasion, the citizens of the Royal Burgh of Wick ask yo Majesty to accept this writing desk and chair as a gift given love and loyalty to our youngest Burgess. We hope that Yo Majesty may rest in Caithness amid the picturesque a changeful panorama of the Pentland Firth, and enjoy pea and relaxation from the exacting duties which are t dedicated and devoted tasks of Royalty.

"We read that Queen Victoria wrote a journal fr Balmoral. Perhaps Your Majesty may write from this de some reminiscences from what we sincerely wish will many visits to the county of Caithness, including the Ro Burgh of Wick."

The Gifts

The desk is a Serpentine front, pedestal type, made Honduras mahogany of modern design, by Mr J. Conr Pringle, hand made by Whytock and Reid, Edinburgh. T armchair, also of mahogany, is based on 18th century sty The seat is covered in blue striped velvet.

Accepting the Freedom, the Queen Mother said:
"I am grateful to you, Provost Leith, for your kind and nerous words and the great honour you have paid me day. To have had conferrred on me the Freedom of Wick , I feel, a symbol of the kindness which I have always found vaiting me in Caithness.
"When on one of my first visits three or four years ago, I und the Castle of Mey, with its long history, its serene auty and its proud setting, faced with the prospect of aving no one able to occupy it, I felt a great wish to eserve, if I could, this ancient dwelling.
"It is too common an experience to find that once a house ecomes deserted, its decay begins, and it is a happiness to e to feel that I have been able to save from such an nworthy fate part of Scotland's heritage.

Beauty of Caithness

"It is a delight to me that I now have a home in Caithness, a ounty of such great beauty, combining as it does the peace nd tranquility of an open and uncrowded countryside with ne rugged glory of a magnificent coastline — the remote etachment of country villages with the busy and independent life of your market towns.
"When I came here, I felt at once at home and among iends, and now believe that I understand something of the reat qualities of those who, through the centuries, have erved your county and our country.
"For I know well that in this northernmost county of this nainland of Scotland, a very wonderful heritage is maintined. It is a product of many generations of brave and ndependent life spent amid the uncertainties of our ntractable climate. From here there springs a breed — dventurous yet wise, strong-willed yet kindly, uncompromsing yet understanding. At home, in all parts of the United Kingdom they have made their mark in every walk of life — n industry and commerce, in crofting and fishing, in eaching, in politics and in the Church.

Citizens Overseas

"But it is not only here that your citizens have shown their rowess. To all parts of our Commonwealth, men from Caithness have gone forth, inspired by a love of adventure, o seek their future in far-off lands. You will find them in the heep farms of Australia, in the ranches of Canada, in the ishing fleets of Newfoundland and in the mines of South Africa. Wherever they may be, you will find that integrity nd singleness of purpose which is so characteristic of the nen of Caithness.
"In times of war, as in times of peace, your citizens are not low to serve their country. Their record of service in your ounty regiment, the Seaforth Highlanders, with its outtanding reputation gained so worthily in battlefields all over he world is well-known. In the Royal Navy and merchant ervice and in the Royal Air Force, this county has more than layed its part.
"I know that in the years since the war, many great evelopments have taken place in your county and in the urgh of Wick and I am most happy today, to have the pportunity of seeing for myself the progress which has been nade in the spheres of Education, the Health Service and Housing. I trust that in the years to come this fine and istoric burgh will go forward in happiness and prosperity.

"Cherished Place"

"May I say, Provost Leith, how deeply touched I am to eceive the beautiful gifts of the desk and chair. I assure you hat they will always have a very cherished place in the Castle of Mey.
"I am indeed glad to be a neighbour of Wick and I most deeply appreciate the single honour of being granted the Freedom of the Royal Burgh." Thereafter, on the call of the Provost, three rousing cheers were given for Wick's youngest Burgess.

Special Feature

As a special feature of the programme, six pupils of Wick High School danced a strathspey entitled "Castle of Mey," the movements of which represented the line of the castle and the turrets. Despite the difficult conditions under which the dance was performed, it was very well executed by the girls and much appreciated by everyone.

The strathspey was specially composed for the occasion by Mrs J. A. Abernethy, physical training instructress at the High School, who also trained the girls for the dance.

The dancers were Misses Margaret Fraser, Alison Banks, Barbara Miller, Hazel Baillie, Christine More and Jean Mackenzie.

Following the singing of the Doxology, the Benediction was pronounced by Rev. W.N. Scott. The gathering then sang the National Anthem, after which the Queen Mother left the Riverside to go to the Station Hotel, where she had lunch with the Town Council and other guests. Before leaving the platform the Royal visitor got another rousing cheer.

At the Old Men's Rest

During the course of her tour of the town, the Queen Mother visited Wick Old Men's Rest and Rosebank Playing Fields. She was accompanied by the Provost and magistrates.

Hundreds of people gathered at the Rest. The crowd was able to watch the approach of the Royal visitor's car and those accompanying her, as they proceeded along Willowbank, down Scalesburn and along The Shore towards the Service Bridge and again as they came round from Martha Terrace along the front of the harbour and up Harbour Terrace.

On arrival at the Rest, the Queen Mother was greeted by Col. Ian McHardy, president of the club, who was presented by the Provost.

Inside the Rest which was tastefully laid out with flowers and model ships, both sail and steam, Mrs McHardy was presented, as was the oldest member 84-year-old Mr Charles Budge, retired cooper, Wellington Street, and members of the committee.

She chatted informally with the committee members, individually and in groups and showed great interest in the premises. She was particularly impressed with the model ships, some of which she examined closely, as well as photographs adorning the walls. Some of them were scenes of the harbour in bygone days and she commented on their clarity of detail.

One of the models which Her Majesty admired was of a naval mine-layer (126), made to scale by the late Mr George Sinclair, cinema projectionist, Seaforth Lodge, Thurso. It was presented to her on behalf of the Club. She told Col McHardy: "I have a grandchild at home who will be very much interested in this."

Her Majesty was most impressed with all she saw in the Rest and commented on the homely atmosphere of the premises and the fine view from its windows.

The Royal visitor then stepped out on to the veranda at the front and chatted to other members and their wives, who were assembled inside the rails, before taking her departure amid cheers from the crowd.

The platform party at the Riverside.

Six pupils of Wick High School dance a strathspey entitled "Castle of Mey"

The Queen Mother and Provost Bessie Leith pause at the entrance of the Station Hotel to admire the beautiful floral display, (Pictured below) before proceeding to lunch with the Town Council and other guests

The Queen Mother accompanied by Provost Bessie Leith, leaving the Station Hotel to tour the town

The Queen Mother was greeted by Col. Ian McHardy (right) when she arrived at the Old Men's Rest

The Queen Mother was most impressed with all she saw in the Rest and commented on the homely atmosphere

The Queen Mother chats with some of the members of the Old Men's Rest

The Queen Mother smilingly bids goodbye to the crowd as she leaves the Old Men's Rest of Pulteneytown

Her Majesty proceeds towards the Playing Fields Pavilion

As she enters the Playing Fields, Wick's youngest Burgess is greeted by Col. J.J. Robertson, honorary vice-president of th Playing Fields Association

Royal Ceremony at Scrabster Harbour

Queen Mother names Thurso's new lifeboat

Arriving at the Harbour accompanied by Viscount Thurso Lord Lieutenant of Caithness and President of the RNLI. The Queen Mother is greeted by cheering crowds

Thurso's new lifeboat, Dunnet Head, the most modern type in the service, donated by the Civil Service Lifeboat Fund at a cost of £35,000, was officially named on Saturday afternoon, 18th August, 1956, by Queen Elizabeth the Queen Mother. The ceremony took place at Scrabster Harbour, where thousands of people had gathered.

It was a day that will be long remembered by the people of Caithness, for in additon to witnessing this Royal event, they saw the arrival in Thurso bay of the Royal yacht Britannia on her way to Leith, with the Queen, Duke of Edinburgh and their family, after their tour of the West of Scotland.

There was a family reunion on board the yacht in the evening when the Queen Mother had dinner with the Royal Family. Later the Britannia proceeded on her voyage to Leith. The Queen was on her way to attend the Edinburgh Festival.

During the lifeboat ceremony, the Queen Mother and others paid well-deserved tribute to Thurso branch of the Royal National Lifeboat Institution for its splendid work in recent years. It was revealed that this year the branch had raised over £1700 as a result of their Lifeboat Week — a proud record indeed.

Long before the ceremony commenced at three o'clock, the quays were packed with people who had come from all parts of the county. Many found an excellent vantage stance on the St. Ola, berthed on the opposite side of the harbour. True, she had a slight list towards the scene, which was all the better for the spectators. The list was due to low tide, although there was a big enough "cargo" to have put the Ola on an even keel, if they had been uniformly distributed!

The Lifeboat Committee and their many assistants had been hard at work preparing for this great event, and it will be many a long day before Scrabster harbour will present the colourful spectacle that was witnessed on Saturday.

The Queen Mother motored to Scrabster from the Castle of Mey, accompanied by Lady Victoria Wemyss, Lady-in-Waiting, and Colonel G. M. Gilliat, Equerry.

Thurso Pipe Band, under acting Pipe-Major John Crowden, preceded the Royal car down the quay. Her Majesty was welcomed by Viscount Thurso, Lord-Lieutenant of Caithness and president of Thurso branch of the R.N.L.I.

The Guard of Honour

Before proceeding to the platform, the Queen Mother inspected the guard of honour, composed of members of the local companies of the Boys' Brigade , Boy Scouts and Girl Guides, under the command of Captain John A. Budge, 1st Thurso Boys' Brigade.

A beautiful bouquet of red roses and white heather was presented to Her Majesty by Miss Maureen Mackenzie, the nine-year-old daughter of Captain Willliam Mackenzie, harbourmaster, Scrabster, and hon. secretary of the lifeboat branch. She received in turn, a box of chocolates and a lifeboat pencil.

The singing of the National Anthem preceded the main programme.

Seafaring Traditions

Introducing the proceedings, Viscount Thurso said that at any time, the launching and christening of a new lifeboat was a milestone in the history of the branch and was a lasting memory for those who participated, but this was particularly the case today for they had to welcome among them, Her Majesty Queen Elizabeth the Queen Mother.

"We have a great pride in our seafaring traditions. These traditions are most fully maintained by our splendid lifeboat and crew. In these little fishing communities here for 100 years we have never lacked for men to undertake the dangerous, hazardous duty in sailing the lifeboat. When a coxswain comes to the end of his time, there is always to be found in this community, a man with the extraordinary qualities of skill and discipline, ready to receive the torch and to maintain, and even add lustre to, the traditions of which we are so proud — the tradition of the Thurso lifeboat men.

"On this occasion — on this lovely warm afternoon — we look down upon the new lifeboat below us and we look up to Queen Elizabeth the Queen Mother and our hearts are full of happiness and pride on this occasion and we do well I think, to begin our proceedings by singing the hymn 'Eternal Father, Strong to Save.' "

The praise was led by the Thurso S.A. Band, the Town Band and the combined church and school choirs.

Thereafter, Sir Eric A. Seal, chairman of the Civil Service Lifeboat Fund, presented the lifeboat to the Institution. It was a great honour for him to represent the donors of this magnificent lifeboat, he said. "I know that she represents the very latest and the very best in lifeboat construction," said Sir Eric.

This was the first Thurso lifeboat to be donated by the Civil Service Lifeboat Fund. The Fund was started 90 yea ago in 1866 and in that period they had presented to th Institution, 31 lifeboats including the Thurso one. The Fu gave to every Civil Service throughout the length a breadth of the land, an opportunity to contribute. The fi lifeboat that the fund paid for 90 years ago, was propelled 10 oars and cost £300, which in those days was a high price f such a boat. Thurso's new boat had a powerful diesel engi and cost more than one hundred times as much as its fi predecessor.

Only the best was good enough for the men who sailed the lifeboats. "Here is a challenge to all of us to raise ev higher our target for the Royal National Lifeboat Instit tion," said Sir Eric. "The Civil Service Lifeboat Fund particularly pleased that their thirty-first lifeboat is to stationed not only in Scotland but here in Thurso."

"Tremendous Need"

"We know that she will have a splendid and gallant cre and we know that there is a tremendous need for a first cla boat in these stormy and turbulent waters of the Pentlar Firth. We know also that she will be backed up in this town Thurso, by one of the most energetic and enthusiast branches that supports the R.N.L.I."

Concluding, he said: "It is with the greatest pleasure tha formally hand over this splendid vessel to the Royal Nation Lifeboat Institution."

Viscount Thurso, in calling upon Commodore the Earl Howe, Chairman of the Institution, to accept the lifebo said he was a direct descendent of Admiral Lord Howe w led his ships to victory on the glorious 1st of June some 1 years ago.

Earl Howe began by recalling that three years ago he h visited Thurso and its lifeboat station. "When I got back London," he said, "I reported to my colleagues on t Committee of Management that Thurso was one of the fine and most efficient stations that I had the opportunity to vis This was due very particularly to a great honorary secreta and to one of the finest coxswains with the lifeboat service round the coast. It was also due to a perfectly wonderf Ladies' Guild and last, but certainly not least, to the gre bulk of the Thurso people."

"Great Strides"

Showing the great strides that Thurso branch had ma within the past few years, he said that in 1951 they had rais £20. Then they decided that that was not enough and form a Ladies' Lifeboat Guild. In the three years following th had raised a total of £3802. This year they had broken records by raising over £1600 during their Lifeboat We (the final figure was over £1700). This wonderful effort w the result of the grand work by the Ladies' Guild backed Captain Mackenzie, secretary, and Coxswain A. Macintos The population of Thurso was 3300 but if they add Scrabster it reached a total of about 5000.

Great Honour

"When Coxswain Macintosh takes her to sea and his cr know well that all Thurso is already in the boat with the said Earl Howe.

"I waited for a long time to pay this humble tribute behalf of the Committee of Management," he said.

In conclusion he said: "It is a great honour to be allowed accept this boat from Sir Eric Seal and that gra organisation the Civil Service Lifeboat Fund. I have t utmost confidence in handing it over to the Thurso bran and to the magnificent chaps who run it."

Many people found an excellent vantage point from the St Ola berthed on the opposite side of the Harbour

Inspecting the guard of honour, composed of the Boys' Brigade, Boy Scouts and Girl Guides

Accepting the boat, Captain W. Mackenzie, who is the harbourmaster at Scrabster, as well as hon. secretary of the lifeboat branch, said he felt happy and honoured in being asked to do so. His predecessor as hon. secretary, the late Mr John Miller of Scrabster, was always of the opinion that they would never make the lifeboat as good as the old sailing boat. As a professional seaman, Captain Mackenzie said he had agreed with Mr Miller to a certain extent. Mr Miller always thought the last ship was always the best ship. That did not apply to their new lifeboat, however. "We have a magnificent new boat here," he said.

"It gives me great pleasure to accept it, not only on behalf of the Thurso branch, but also on behalf of the people from Cape Wrath to Duncansby Head, because you all have a share in her judging by last week's results."

Captain Mackenzie then read four greetings telegrams wishing the Thurso branch every success on this auspicious occasion. They were from the Cromarty Branch, Longhope Branch, Orkney Mainland Ladies Guild, and Mr William McIvor, former lifeboat mechanic.

The New Boat

A description of the Dunnet Head was given by Commander T. G. Michael More, chief inspector of lifeboats.

The new vessel is a cabin motor lifeboat, 47 feet long and 12 feet 9 inches in beam. On service, with crew and gear on board, she weighs 22¾ tons. She is launched down a slipway. Her steering position is amidships and enclosed. She is divided into nine watertight compartments, which are fitted with 236 air-cases, and below the engine room floor there is a double bottom to make her even more unsinkable. Her twin screws are driven by two 60 h.p. Gardiner diesel engines, which give her a full speed of 8¼ knots, and she carries enough fuel to be able to travel 278 miles at this speed without refuelling. All engine manoeuvring and operating controls are arranged for working from inside the steering position, and no member of the crew is required in the engine room while the boat is under way.

She carries a crew of eight, and in rough weather can take 95 people on board. She has a deck cabin , with a paraffin pressure cooker, and below decks, a second cabin with electric fans for ventilating it. She is fitted with radio telephone, for which there is a separate compartment in the deck cabin, a loud hailer, and an oil spray to make smoother the water round the wreck. She carries a line-throwing pistol, an electric searchlight, and a daylight signalling lamp.

A comprehensive vote of thanks to all who had taken part in the proceedings and in organising the event, was proposed by Lord Saulton, chairman of The Scottish Lifeboat Council.

After Rev. D. C. Alexander, minister of St. Peter's and St. Andrew's Church, dedicated the lifeboat, the assembly rose to sing the hymn "O God our help in ages past".

The Crew

In addition to Coxswain Angus Macintosh, the crew of the lifeboat are: Second Coxswain David Thomson; Engineer, Donald Bews; 2nd Engineer Angus Reid; Bowman, Donald Mackay; Signaller, Gilbert Reid; R.T. Operator, Alexander Thomson; Spare Hand, James Smith.

In naming the new lifeboat the Queen Mother said: "It gives me great pleasure to be here today at the naming ceremony of this magnificent new lifeboat. As a lifeboat station, Thurso has a record of which the citizens of this burgh, and indeed the whole of Scotland can be justifiabl proud.

"Since 1860 when the station was established, more tha 500 people have been rescued by Thurso's lifeboats fro being lost at sea. Thurso has also, I know, a remarkab record in raising money for the lifeboat service.

"Three years ago the Committee of Management of th Institution singled out your town for a special letter of thank and congratulations for the work done in raising money fc this great voluntary service, and I have been deepl impressed to hear of the splendid result of your latest effor

"With the advance of science and many new technical aic to navigation, it might be thought that the need for th lifeboat service would be growing less, but this is far from th case. All round our coast there is always present peril, t those who go down to the sea in ships and the call upon th service is as great as ever.

"I feel certain that the fine tradition of going out to rescu others without thought of self and of supporting the men wh do so, will long continue to flourish in Thurso.

"I now name this new lifeboat, Dunnet Head. (Civ Service No. 36). May God bless all who sail in her."

Three rousing cheers were given the Queen Mother, o the call of Lord Thurso.

In proposing a vote of thanks to Her Majesty for th gracious manner in which she had performed the ceremon Provost John Sinclair, chairman of the Thurso lifeb branch, said: "This is indeed a memorable day in the histo of Thurso. The presence of Your Majesty shows the ve great royal interest the members of the Royal Family take the work of the institution. On behalf of the Institution, th local committee and the crew of the lifeboat, I humb tender to Your Majesty our loyal thanks for so graciousl coming here this afternoon and naming our lifeboat th Dunnet Head.

"Having your home on the shores of the Pentland Firt may I respectfully suggest that it is most appropriate that Caithness lady should launch a lifeboat on its mission mercy in saving lives at sea."

He asked them to accord Her Majesty their very since and grateful thanks for graciously and charmingly settir their new lifeboat on its journey.

Provost Sinclair then presented the Queen Mother with box of chocolates on behalf of the Institution to mark th pleasant and happy afternoon.

Royal Gesture

Following the ceremony, the Queen Mother boarded t new lifeboat and went for a 20-minute run in Thurso Ba She took the wheel for a 10-minute spell. While she w aboard, she gave a sprig of white heather to Coxswa Macintosh and the members of the crew from her bouquet a gesture which was much appreciated by the me Altogether she was delighted with her trip in the boat.

On Her Majesty's return, a number of presentations to place, after which the official guests were entertained to te

At the tea, the Queen Mother cut a beautiful iced-cak decorated with a model of the lifeboat. The cake was ma by Mr J. A. Johnstone, St. Clair Bakery, Thurso. A repli of the cake was presented to Her Majesty.

Meanwhile, most of the crowd proceeded back to Thur to await the arrival of Her Majesty who was scheduled visit Thurso's St. Peter's Church, built in 1832 and recen renovated and redecorated, before being opened for pub worship on Sunday.

The Queen Mother names the new lifeboat, releasing a bottle of champagne which broke on the vessel's bows

A general view of Scrabster Harbour, showing the thronged quayside. On the right of the picture is the new lifeboat, the Dunnet Head. She is escorted by the Longhope lifeboat, the Thomas MaCann.

The Dunnet Head Lifeboat and crew standing at attention during the ceremony

The Royal Yacht Britannia anchored in Thurso Bay

Family Reunion Aboard The Royal Yacht Britannia

Her Majesty spent about a quarter of an hour inside the ıilding and in expressing her admiration, she said she was ırticularly struck by the curved roof, stained glass windows ıd the general effect of the internal decoration.

The church organist, Mr Gavin Lafferty, the 45-year-old usic master in Miller Academy, was asked by Her Majesty play the organ and he chose two pieces, one from Bach ıd the other from Handel. The Queen Mother admired ery much the tone of the organ, one of the finest in the ountry.

The crowd were still waiting when Her Majesty left the urch and she got a great cheer as she left by car for the astle of Mey.

Britannia Arrives

All day there had been rumours that the Royal yacht ritannia, on its way to Leith after the Queen's triumphant ur in the Western Isles, would put into Thurso bay that ght and that the Queen, the Duke of Edinburgh, Prince harles and Princess Anne and other members of the Royal mily would come ashore as they did last year.

Rumour was right to some extent. The Britannia, escorted the destroyer, Orwell, arrived at Scrabster Roads at 7.30. ong before then, crowds of people had gathered at the ırbour, taking up vantage points on the quays and ındreds more were hurrying towards the scene.

This was something extra for the sightseers who had ready enjoyed an exciting day. Most of them hoped to see e Queen and the Royal family but they were to be sappointed.

At eight o'clock, the Queen Mother arrived by car from e Castle of Mey, accompanied by Lady Victoria Wemyss ıd Col. G.M. Gilliat. Shortly before that, a Royal barge ıd left the Britannia and was waiting at the quay to take the ueen Mother to the Britannia for dinner with the Royal mily.

The weather had held and in fact it was a beautiful night. he bay, which had been calm all day, was slightly ruffled ith a north-easterly wind.

Many people remained at the harbour, hoping that some embers of the Royal family, particularly Prince Charles ıd Princess Anne, might return with the Queen Mother.

Princess Margaret

It was 10.45, however, before the barge returned and ere were still hundreds of people waiting on the quay when e Queen Mother came ashore. Accompanying her in the ırge was Princess Margaret, who received a great ovation hen she was recognised. The Princess returned to the yacht ıd the Queen Mother motored back to Mey where eparations had been made for greeting the Britannia as she ıssed the Castle on her way through the Pentland Firth.

Large numbers of people had gathered on the shore at Mey and the vicinity to watch the scene and they were rewarded by seeing a fine display.

Floodlit and presenting a perfect silhouette against the dark sea, the Royal yacht, close inshore, moved slowly past.

Castle Floodlit

The Castle was also floodlit and to add to the colour and brilliancy of the scene, rockets and flares were sent off from the grounds by members of the Wick Coastguard staff under Commander H.L. Gilbert. The Britannia and Orwell also sent off rockets.

Greetings were exchanged by signal between the Castle and the yacht.

The Queen Mother and her guests were out on the shore behind the Castle. Delighted with the termination of the day's programme. Her Majesty thanked the coastguards for their services and also Mr Robert Finlayson, electrician, Wick, who was responsible for floodlighting the castle. Augmenting the lighting were two searchlights provided by the Coastguard.

Guard of Honour at Church

The 1st Thurso Company and 1st Castletown Company of the Boys' Brigade formed a guard of honour at Canisbay Old Church when the Queen Mother attended the noon service on Sunday. Captain John A. Budge, Thurso, was in command of the guard. The Castletown Company paraded under their captain, Mr G. Macleod.

Her Majesty was accompanied by Commander C.G. Vyner and Lady Doris Vyner and attended by Lady Victoria Wemyss and Col. G.M. Gilliat. She was welcomed by Rev. Nigel Johnstone, who conducted the service. There was a large congregation.

The Queen Mother spoke to several of the boys and was particularly interested in their badges.

Visit to Art Show

The Royal visitor left Caithness on Tuesday afternoon, flying from Wick Airport in a Viking of the Queen's flight. Earlier in the day, she paid a visit to the annual show being held by the Society of Caithness Artists in the Miller Academy, Thurso, and was greatly interested in the various exhibits.

At the Airport to bid good-bye to the Queen Mother, were Viscount Thurso, Lord Lieutenant, and Brig. G.D.K. Murray, Vice-Lieutenant. Others present were the Hon. Robin M. Sinclair, Mr G.T. Stanley, commandant of the Northern Group of Airports, Mr T.T. Sommerville, airport manager, and Mr J.W. Georgeson, chief constable.

Her Majesty was travelling to Aberdeenshire where she rejoined the Royal family and was in time for Princess Margaret's birthday party that night at Balmoral Castle.

Her Majesty acknowledges the cheers of the crowd before entering St Peter's Church

The Queen Mother at the annual show of Caithness artists in the Miller Academy, Thurso

DECEMBER 1956

Thurso's new lifeboat destroyed by fire

Modern Vessel Cost £35,000

One of the latest types of vessels in service on the British ast, Thurso's new lifeboat, the Dunnet Head, was totally stroyed in a blaze which also gutted the lifeboat shed and ar at Scrabster on Monday morning 10th December. The unnet Head was officially named by Queen Elizabeth the ueen Mother at a ceremony on 18th August.

The outbreak occurred in the early morning and the alarm as given by Mr David McBay, assistant harbourmaster at rabster, who saw sparks coming from the lifeboat shed.

Captain Wm. Mackenzie, harbourmaster, who is also ecretary of the local Lifeboat Branch, was in the harbour ffice at the time and he ran to the scene.

He found the whole workshop end of the shed ablaze. aptain Mackenzie said later: "I opened the shed door with e idea of launching the lifeboat with or without a crew, but here was nothing I could do."

Thurso Fire Brigade were summoned and Wick Fire rigade was called out to help. The flames, however, had wept swiftly through the pitch pine lined building which was blaze and nothing could be done to save it.

Crowds of people gathered on the spot but had to look on elplessly. Among them was Provost John Sinclair, chair-nan of the Lifeboat Branch.

The launching gear, winch and workshop were all destroyed.

It was only two days previously — on Saturday — that the lifeboat was launched for its half-yearly trials, following which Mr Alex. Cursiter, and R.N.L.I., northern district engineer, told Captain Mackenzie that he congratulated all concerned on the efficiency of the Thurso station and on the performance of the boat.

The Dunnet Head was sent to Scrabster last January to replace the former lifeboat, the H.C.J., which had given 26 years' service. Built at Cowes, the Dunnet Head was fitted with the latest life saving and navigational equipment, including an echo-sounder. She had twin 60h.p. Gardiner diesel engines, capable of producing a top speed of nearly nine knots, and she carried enough fuel to be able to travel 278 miles at this speed, without refuelling.

A cabin motor lifeboat, she was 47 feet in length and 12 feet 9 inches in beam.

The coxswain of the Dunnet Head, Skipper Angus Mackintosh of the Thurso seine-net boat, Two Boys, was out fishing when the fire occurred. He saw the smoke but had no idea it was the lifeboat shed that was on fire.

The James Macphee, which was previously stationed as a relief boat at Scrabster, had been sent north to cover the Thurso station's operational area.

The ill-fated Dunnet Head Lifeboat (Foreground)

A black five class 5MT 460 steam locomotive arrives at Georgemas Station pulling the Royal coaches (Pictured below).

Brigadier G.D.K. Murray, Vice-Lieutenant of Caithness, welcomes the Queen Mother as she steps from the Royal coach a Georgemas Station.

Royal Visitor at Local Art Show

'he Queen Mother viewing the exhibits; she is accompanied by Major James B. Simpson Wick (left) and Sheriff D.B. Keith Kirkwall, (a native of Thurso).

The Queen Mother visited the Miller Academy, Thurso, 'here the Society of Caithness Artists held their annual xhibition. This was her Majesty's third successive visit to ne Society's shows.

Following a ten-day holiday in Caithness, Queen :lizabeth the Queen Mother left the county on Tuesday 20th ugust, to join the Queen and the Royal family at Balmoral. ler Majesty flew in a Viking of the Queen's Flight which left Vick Airport shortly after 3 p.m. She was accompanied by Lady Hyde, Lady-in-Waiting and Colonel Martin Gilliat, Secretary.

Although it was sunny, a strong westerly wind swept the airfield. The Queen Mother wore a dove grey coat with white hat.

Before boarding the plane, the Royal visitor spoke to Mr A.M. Campbell, airport commandant, and Mr W.D. Reid, airport manager.

The Queen Mother said: "I have had a very nice holiday in Caithness."

On Her arrival at St Peter's, Her Majesty is welcomed by the minister, Rev. D.C. Alexander. Below, the Royal visitor leaves afte the service.

Queen Mother to attend Princess Margaret's birthday party

Queen Elizabeth the Queen Mother, who is on holiday in 'aithness, went to London on Monday 11th August, to meet rincess Margaret, who was returning the following day om her tour of Canada which has been most successful.

Her Majesty returned to Caithness yesterday (Thursday) 4th August, flying from London in a Heron of the Queen's light. She was accompanied by Lady Victoria Wemyss, ady-in-Waiting, and Colonel Martin Gilliat, Private ecretary.

When the plane touched down at Wick Airport at 3.20, ver 100 people had gathered, many of them being holiday-akers. The spectators were hoping that Princess Margaret as along with the Queen Mother but the Princess had not avelled north.

It was a warm, sunny day and Her Majesty chatted for ome time with Mr G.T. Stanley, airport commandant, and Mr W.D. Reid, airport manager, who were there to welcome her.

On entering her private car to travel to the Castle of Mey, the Queen Mother smiled and waved to the crowd.

At Church

On Sunday, the Royal Visitor attended the midday services in St. Andrew's Church, Thurso. She was accompanied by Commander G.C. Vyner and Lady Doris Vyner, Dunnet, Lady Victoria Wemyss and the Hon. Mrs John Gilmour, Ladies-in-Waiting, and Colonel Gilliat.

The Queen Mother is expected to leave Caithness on Wednesday to join the Queen and the Royal family at Balmoral and on the following day she will attend Princess Margaret's birthday party.

The Queen Mother arrives at Wick Airport for her holiday at the Castle of Mey

First official visit to Canisbay Old Churc

This was the first time that the Queen Mother had worshipped in Canisbay Church, which had been vacant for over a year. During the vacancy, the Queen Mother, when in residence at the Castle, attended one of the churches in Thurso.

Shopping in Thurso

The Queen Mother paid a visit to J. Miller Calder, house furnishers, Thurso, on Tuesday morning 7th August. She spent about half an hour inspecting antiques and curios displayed in the main showroom. Only a handful of people saw the Royal visitor arrive but by the time she was ready to leave, after making a few purchases, a large crowd had gathered.

Queen Elizabeth the Queen Mother, who is at present o holiday in Caithness, motored from the Castle of Mey o Sunday to attend the noon service in Canisbay Old Churc where she was welcomed by the new minister, Rev. Geor Bell.

Her Majesty was accompanied by Commander C.C Vyner and Lady Doris Vyner, Lady Hyde, Lady-in-Waitin and Sir Arthur Penn, her Financial Secretary.

Few people were about when the Royal visitor arrive She was wearing a light tweed coat with pink feathered h and carried a fur. There was a large attendance of t congregation, although the day was cold and blustery.

The Queen Mother bids goodbye to the minister, Rev. George Bell, after attending the service in Canisbay Old Church on Sunday A young spectator is intensely interested

"Wait for me!" The Queen Mother, seated in the rear of her chauffeur driven Rover, was most amused at this incident, captured by John Adams at Wick Airport. Apparently the Queen Mother's corgi decided to go "walkies"; but for the acute observation of the police officer, (pictured above) the Royal corgi may well have spent the night at Wick Police Station - for safe keeping of course.

AUGUST 1959

Queen Mother Picnics on Stroma

Mrs Manson, son Andrew and the family pet dog Spy welcome strangers.

Since she came north on Friday 7th August, for a holiday at the Castle of Mey, Queen Elizabeth the Queen Mother has enjoyed perfect weather. It has been warm with bright sunshine most of the time.

The Royal visitor travelled from London by train, which reached Georgemas Junction at 2 p.m. on Friday. She was accompanied by Lady Hyde, Lady-in-Waiting, and Col. Martin Gilliat, Secretary. Her Majesty wore a royal blue coat and white straw hat with pale blue spotted veil.

Waiting on the platform to welcome the Queen Mother were Commander C.G. Vyner and Lady Doris Vyner, the House of the Northern Gate, Dunnet.

Mr Alan Yeaman, Inverness, district traffic superintendent, and Mr James Gunn, station master, were also present.

Before leaving the platform, Her Majesty waved goodbye to the train crew — Driver David Miller, a native of Wick, Fireman James Henderson and Guard David Ross (all of Inverness).

The Queen Mother left in her private car for the Castle of Mey.

At Church

On Sunday, the Queen Mother attended the noon service in Canisbay Old Church where she was welcomed by the minister, Rev. George Bell. The church was crowded an the congregation included a number of visitors on holiday i the district.

Picnic on Stroma

The Queen Mother took the opportunity on Tuesday 11t August, of visiting Stroma Island. This was the first time sh had ever been on it since she purchased the Castle of Mey Her Majesty was welcomed by the only family, apart fron the lighthouse staff, now living on Stroma — Mr and Mr Andrew Manson and their two sons.

The Royal visitor crossed from the mainland in the Thurs seine net motor boat, Primula, the co-owners of which ar Skipper Angus Mackintosh and Provost John Sinclair. Th Provost was aboard the Primula when it set sail from Phillip harbour, which is situated near the Castle of Mey.

The Queen Mother was accompanied by Lady Hyde, Col Martin Gilliat, Commander Vyner and Lady Doris Vyner. I was a beautiful warm day and after sightseeing on the islan the party picnicked there.

After sailing round the island, they passed through th tidal race, known locally as the Swelkie.

The Primula later returned to Thurso. On the way, He Majesty had a perfect view of her Castle from the sea. Th party was entertained to tea aboard the fishing boat.

Queen Mother on Holiday in Caithness

The Queen Mother arrived in Caithness on Friday. The ·evious day, she had celebrated her 60th birthday at ·larence House. Her Majesty flew from London in a Heron ' the Queen's Flight, which touched down at Wick Airport ·ortly before 4 p.m.

A large crowd of people, including many holidaymakers, ·ad gathered at the airport to watch the arrival of the Royal ·sitor.

The day was warm and sunny with the maximum ·mperature touching 60. The Queen Mother wore a royal ·ue coat over a light blue dress and an off-white hat.

Her Majesty was accompanied by the Duke and Duchess ' Beaufort. Lady Hyde, Lady-in-Waiting, was in attend- ·nce, and Col. Martin Gilliat, Private Secretary, also ·avelled in the plane.

Waiting at the airport to welcome the Queen Mother, ·ere Commander C.G. Vyner and Lady Doris Vyner.

As the Queen Mother stepped from the plane, the crowd ·neered and waved. Her private car was waiting to take her ·the Castle of Mey. The Duke and Duchess of Beaufort ·avelled with her.

On Sunday, Her Majesty attended the noon service in Canisbay Old Church. Her guests, the Duke and Duchess of Beaufort, who were staying at the Castle for the first time, accompanied her. Others in the party were Lady Hyde, Colonel Martin Gilliat, and Captain Peter Aird, Equerry.

Although the weather was dull, conditions were pleasant at the time. There was a large congregation of local people and visitors.

On the arrival and departure of Her Majesty, a large number of people assembled outside the church. The service was conducted by Rev. George Bell, minister, who welcomed the Royal visitor and party when they arrived.

Visit to Thurso

Hundreds of visitors and local people crowded around the Queen Mother on Wednesday morning when she made a surprise visit to her two favourite shops in Thurso. Seconds after the Royal visitor's car had appeared in the town's main streets, movie cameras, box cameras and anything that could record the event, were produced from nowhere.

Her Majesty wore a light blue costume with hat to match. She first visited the premises of Miller Calder, furnishers, and then walked through the crowds to The Ship's Wheel antique shop, 20 yards down the road.

Her Majesty leaving the church, accompanied by the Duchess of Beaufort (left) and Lady Hyde, Lady-in-Waiting. The minister, Rev George Bell, is seen speaking to other members of the party.

AUGUST 1961

Queen Mother on annual holiday in Caithness

Queen Elizabeth the Queen Mother is spending a fortnight's holiday in Caithness. She arrived on Thursday 3rd August last week, travelling from London in a Heron of the Queen's Flight. She was accompanied by Mrs John Mulholland, Lady-in-Waiting, and Major John Griffin, Equerry.

A small crowd of people was at Wick Airport when th Royal visitor arrived about 4 p.m. Her Majesty wore a ligl blue coat with hat to match. She was welcomed at the Airpo by Mr G.T. Stanley, commandant of the Northern Group.

From the Airport, the Queen Mother travelled to Mey i her private car.

AUGUST 1961

Queen and Royal Family

Large crowds see Her Majesty arrive and depart from Scrabster

Sunday 13th August, was a Royal day in Caithness. Her Iajesty the Queen along with the Duke of Edinburgh, rince Charles and Princess Anne and a party of friends ame ashore at Scrabster from the Royal yacht Britannia to isit Queen Elizabeth the Queen Mother at the Castle of Iey; earlier in the day, the Queen Mother attended the orenoon service in Wick Old Parish Church.

The Queen's visit was not unexpected, as the Royal yacht as on its way from the west coast to the northeast of cotland, where Her Majesty had a number of official ngagements on Monday.

The Royal party landed at Scrabster at 2.30 p.m. It had een warm and sunny all day and hundreds of people athered on the pier to see the visitors as they disembarked om the Royal launch. The Britannia had anchored in hurso Bay, close inshore.

The Queen was attended by the Countess of Leicester, ady-in-Waiting, and the party, which totalled 14, included rince George and Princess Sophie of Hanover and their ree children.

They were met at Scrabster by Colonel Martin Gilliat, the Queen Mother's secretary, and Commander C.G. Vyner.

The Queen wore a suit and coat to match of grey blue tweed faced with off-white, a rose pink sweater and a blue and white headsquare. Prince Philip was dressed in a checked sports jacket and dark grey flannel trousers. Prince Charles had a heavy sweater and jeans, while Princess Anne wore a shower-proof jerkin, blue blouse and corduroy trousers.

Her Majesty, Prince George and Princess Sophie travelled in the Queen Mother's private car to Mey, 14 miles distant. Prince Philip drove the children in a Land Rover which had been landed from the Royal yacht in a rubber pontoon earlier in the day.

Along the whole route between Scrabster and Mey, cars and people were lined to watch the visitors pass.

At the Castle of Mey, the party had afternoon tea with the Queen Mother. Much of the time ashore was spent on the beach behind the Castle, where the children thoroughly enjoyed themselves playing on the sands.

As she steps on to the pier, Her Majesty is greeted by Colonel Gilliat, the Queen Mother's secretary

AUGUST 1961

Visit to the Castle of Mey

The visitors returned to Scrabster at 7 p.m. Unfortunately, the weather had broken. A light drizzle had set in, but by the time the party arrived at the pier there was a lull and the rain stopped.

Despite the weather, the crowd was larger than in the afternoon. Quiet and orderly, the spectators were delighted to be there to see the Queen and the Royal family and their friends. The arrangements made by the police, assisted by the coastguards, gave the crowd ample room and scope in such limited space to view the scene.

Before leaving to board the launch, Her Majesty spoke for a few minutes with Mr J.W. Georgeson, chief constable.

As soon as the Queen and the party were aboard, the crowd pressed forward to the edge of the quay for a last glimpse. They cheered loudly as the launch sped out of the harbour on its way to the Britannia.

Fireworks Display

The Royal yacht left Scrabster Roads at 9.30 p.m. and as she slowly cruised past the Castle of Mey they could see the Castle floodlit and the display of fireworks at the rear terrace. The Britannia, also floodlit for the occasion, responded with a pyrotechnic display from the deck.

Standing outside the Castle, the Queen Mother and guests had the Royal yacht under view for almost half an hour. Many motorists had gone to vantage points along the Dunnet-John O'Groats road to watch the scene.

The Queen Mother attended the forenoon service in Wic Old Parish Church on Sunday. She drove from the Castle Mey in her private car. It was a warm, sultry day. H Majesty wore a light coat of royal blue and hat to match.

She was attended by Lady Fermoy and was accompanie by Lady Doris Vyner, Commander C.G. Vyner, Sir Edwar Fielden. Commodore of the Queen's Flight; Colonel Marti Gilliat, secretary, and Major John Griffin, Press secretary

A large crowd of people gathered outside the church await the arrival of the Royal visitor. The church was almo full.

At the entrance, Her Majesty was welcomed by t minister, Rev. W. Nethercote Scott, Provost Willia Dunnett, and Mr James Wares, session clerk.

As she left the church to go to her waiting car, Wick Gir Pipe Band played the "Queen Elizabeth March."

Five-week-old Margaret A. Ferguson, daughter of Mr an Mrs Leslie Ferguson, 5 Mey Terrace, Thurso, was baptise in the church by Mr Scott following the service and th Queen Mother's departure.

Below: The Castle of Mey in all its floodlit splendour

AUGUST 1961

Queen Mother Visits Dounreay Atomic Station

Her Majesty Inspects Plant and New Thurso Hostel

Queen Elizabeth the Queen Mother paid an official visit) the Dounreay Experimental Reactor Establishment, pending more than three hours at the station.

With her usual charm, she turned a formal tour into a omely visit, putting everyone at ease. Her Majesty's vident interest in everything she saw, delighted the atomic hiefs and those in charge of the various departments. For er part, the Queen Mother must have appreciated the moothness of the arrangements made for her tour and, idging by the questions she put, she took full advantage of he knowledge of the experts on the spot.

Her Majesty, who was accompanied by Lady Fermoy, ady-in-Waiting, was met at the station by Brigadier Sir eith Murray, Vice-Lieutenant of Caithness, who presented ir Roger Makins, chairman of the United Kingdom Atomic nergy Authority, and Dr Robert Hurst, director of)ounreay.

Afterwards, Dr Hurst presented Lady Makins, Mrs Hurst, Ar T.A. Parry (deputy director of Dounreay), and Mr J.L. hillips (head of the reactor division).

Dr Hurst and Mr Phillips described briefly the main features of the Dounreay fast reactor and outlined the progress made in overcoming certain difficulties incurred during the commission period.

The engineering modifications designed to overcome these difficulties were completed and the reactor became operational again on 14th August, and the effectiveness of these modifications will now be intensively tested.

Later, the Royal visitor entered the reactor control room, where she was invited to press a button to give a demonstration on how to increase the operating power of the reactor.

Members of the staff presented to Her Majesty were Mr K.J. Henry, fast reactor project manager; Mr J. Allen, operations manager; and Mr G.R. Cullington, shift manager on duty.

The Queen Mother pictured with Dr Hurst (centre) Director of Dounreay, at the start of Her official tour of Dounreay Experimental Reactor Establishment

Next, the Queen Mother saw the reactor in operating conditions. She ascended the giant sphere by lift. Almost half an hour was spent there, Her Majesty showing special interest in the operations and putting a number of questions to the personnel on duty. They were Mr J. Kirk of the operating staff, Mr J.B. Pearce and Mr R. Jones of the maintenance and engineering staff, Mr B. McGrory and Mr S. Ramsay, chairman and secretary respectively of the Shop Stewards Committee.

On leaving the sphere, the Royal visitor in turn saw two sections of the laboratory and plant division — the highly active metallurgical caves and the fast reactor fuel fabrication.

Metallurgical Caves

In the metallurgical caves, Mr A. McIntosh, head of the division, described the two main functions of the division — the manufacture and reprocessing of fuel elements for the two reactors at Dounreay, and the development and design of advanced fuels for future fast reactors. The examination of irradiated specimens of advanced fuels is carried out in the caves, where they are contained behind several feet of concrete and viewed through special shielded windows. Handling is by manipulators working through the concrete.

The Royal visitor saw how these examinations were carried out and met some of the men responsible. They were Dr S.A. Cottrell, manager of the radioactive examination group, Dr K. Swanson, and Mr E. Edmonds, scientists in charge of the building. Mr J. McGivern, secretary of the local Whitley Council, was also presented.

In the fuel fabrication plant, the Queen Mother saw two stages of the manufacture of fuel elements for the fast reactor. Here she met Dr D.S. Oliver, manager of the fuel element development group, Mr M. Macphee, operations manager, and Mr H. Disbury, principal process superviso

Her Majesty had lunch in the director's dining-roor Among those present were Colonel Martin J. Gilliat, h Private Secretary, Major John Griffin, Equerry, La Fermoy, Sir Keith Murray, Sir Roger and Lady Makin Captain H.A. Kidd, commanding officer of the Admiral Reactor Testing Establishment, Dr and Mrs Hurst, M Parry, Mr Phillips, Mr McIntosh, Dr S.M.B. Hill (head the health and safety division), Mr W.J. Greig (reside engineer) and Mr D.M. Carmichael, general secretary.

Visit to Hostel

The Queen Mother left Dounreay in the early afterno to visit Naver House Hostel, which was built at a cost about £70,000 and is situated on the Atomic Authority housing estate at Thurso. She was shown over the premis by Dr Hurst. The hostel is managed by the Y.M.C.A. behalf of the Authority.

The Y.M.C.A. manager is Mr James Garioch. He w presented to Her Majesty. Mr Garioch resides about seve miles from Ballater and has often seen the Royal family. Th first time he met the Queen Mother was in 1945 when he w Senior Sergeant-Major of the King's Guard at Sandringha when he was serving with the Gordon Highlanders.

Two Dounreay apprentices were also presented. The were 19-year-old David Oag, a third-year locally recruite craft apprentice, who recently resided on the farm of Ea Mey, quite near the Castle of Mey; and 19-year-old Mervy Skidmore, a first-year student apprentice from Yatto North Somerset.

A large crowd of people who were waiting outside th hostel to see the Queen Mother arrive, were still there wh she left and gave her a loud cheer.

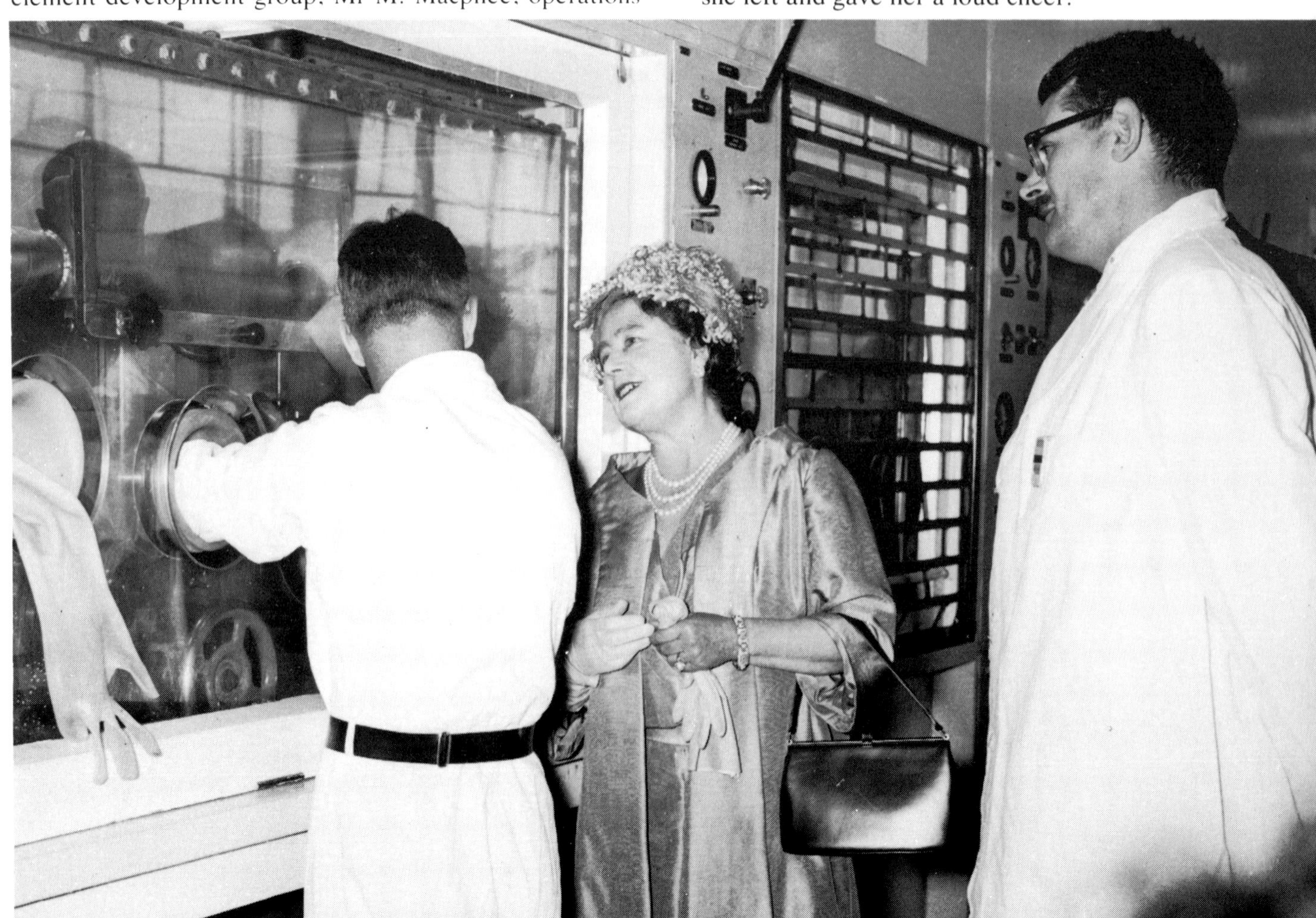

The Queen Mother chats to a scientific officer handling manipulators through a glove box contained behind several feet concrete

Her Majesty the Queen Mother in the Corridors of Power, Dounreay

September 1961: The gardens with the Castle in the background. The Castle gardener, Mr J. Sinclair, is seen in conversation with another well-known gardener,

Rain marred county's best organised show

Cheering crowds greet the Queen Mother as she tours the field

Incessant rain, driven by a strong north-westerly wind, oiled Caithness Agricultural Society's 122nd show, held at e Riverside, Wick, on Saturday 4th August. It was one of e worst days ever experienced by the Society, affecting the tendance seriously — it was only a third of the usual crowd and the sports programme in the afternoon had to be andoned because of ground conditions.

In size, scope and organisation, the show promised to be e best yet, as was evident to all who visited the field. It was sheartening for all concerned that the weather broke — ith storms over land and sea. In the circumstances it was markable that so many people turned up. They did not gret it. They saw Queen Elizabeth the Queen Mother, who as celebrating her 62nd birthday, touring the field in that racious and happy manner which endears her to all, as if the un was shining. It was an inspiration to the crowd and she as cheered wherever she went.

Royal Thanks

Her Majesty realised, too, how much time and energy had een expended in preparing the show. In a letter to Mr ames S. Bruce, Society president, Sir Ralph Anstruther, easurer, wrote that, despite the weather, the Queen lother greatly enjoyed the show and sent her warmest ppreciation to all those whose hard work and enthusiasm ırned a disappointing day into the success it became.

She expressed thanks for the admirable arrangements for er visit, and was grateful for the pavilion, which she much dmired, and also the decorations.

For this special occasion the pavilion and stands were ecorated with floral designs. These, which were much dmired, were the work of Miss Beatrice Simpson, Wick.

Decorations inside the pavilion were provided by Mr James Bruce.

It was a trying day for the officials, committee members and especially the stock attendants, who had been on constant duty since early morning. They, and all who were concerned with the show, rose to the occasion, triumphing over the adverse conditions.

Caravans were used as quarters, offices and for general purposes to a great extent instead of tents, and they demonstrated their value. In every sense they are an improvement, and it is obvious that they have staked their claim for the future. They can be moved and sited easily.

The local firms of Nicolson and Wood (Caravans), Ltd., Wick, and Capital Caravans, Inverness (in association with Park Motors, Wick), had stands displaying vans, and each had a number in use on the ground. Nicolson and Wood struck on the happy idea of playing and recording of musical items by local artistes and a commentary.

From Queen Victoria's Bouquet

The Society presented the Queen Mother with a birthday bouquet which she received at the Castle of Mey on the morning of the Show. It was supplied by Miss Beatrice Simpson, the Flower Centre, Wick.

As part of the foliage, there was a sprig of myrtle from a piece which was in Queen Victoria's wedding bouquet.

The Duchess of Sutherland of that time was one of the Queen's bridesmaids, and she kept a sprig of myrtle which later came into the possession of Mrs D.R. Simpson, Fernbank, grandmother of Miss Beatrice Simpson.

This sprig was kept in a pot in the conservatory at Fernbank and the plant is still growing.

Wet day at the County Show: The Queen Mother prepares for the inclement weather.

From this point, the Royal visitor toured the ground in a jeep. First she went to the cattle pens and then to the sheep where judging was proceeding. The chief sheep steward, Mr Ben S. Mackay, Geiselittle, and the chief cattle steward, Mr John Allan, Gillock, conducted her round the pens.

The Queen Mother spent a considerable time discussing the merits of the entries, showing that she had no little knowledge of stock. She was struck by the sturdy strength of the Caithness cattle. In conversation with 80-year-old Mr James G. Nicol, judge of the Aberdeen-Angus cattle, she found that he had won a Coronation Medal for his champion heifer at the Smithfield Show in 1953.

Her Majesty had 10 entries at the show — one in the cattle sections and nine in the sheep. She won a first prize for her bull, Invader of Durran, and three awards for sheep.

Sir Ralph Anstruther was also delighted to learn that a pen of three gimmers from his farm at Watten Mains had taken a third prize. The manager is Mr David G. Gunn, the Society secretary.

As the Queen Mother moved about the field from point to point she was followed by an enthusiastic crowd.

Shortly before one o'clock, she left to lunch at Ackergill Tower as the guest of Sir George Duff-Dunbar.

Afternoon Session

Returning to the show in the early afternoon, the Royal visitor was given a warm reception from the spectators whose numbers had greatly increased, although it was still raining heavily. She proceeded to the pavilion, from which she saw the parade of prize-winning stock.

Afterwards, Her Majesty presented Long Service Medals to two farmworkers and the principal trophies to successful exhibitors.

The farmservants were Mr Thomas Sutherland, 43 years' service on Dirlot, Rumsdale and Dalnaglettan farms, and at present in the employment of Viscount Thurso; and Mr John Campbell, 30 years' service as cattleman at Watten Mains, now in the employment of Sir Ralph Anstruther.

The storm was at its worst when the Queen Mother arriv at the show entrance. Nevertheless, there was a fairly lar group which had gathered facing the driving rain, to give t Royal visitor a welcome.

Her Majesty, who was accompanied by Sir Ral Anstruther and Lady Fermoy, was met by Brigadier S Keith Murray, Vice-Lieutenant of Caithness, who w accompanied by Lady Murray, Provost William Dunne Mr James S. Bruce, president of the Society, and Mr Geor Baikie, vice-president.

The Queen Mother then proceeded to the W.R.I. tent see the handicraft and baking exhibits. She was received b Mrs G.D.W. Millikin, president of the County W.R. Federation, who presented her with a bouquet in the W.R. colours — blue, gold and white.

Those presented were Mrs I.M. Polson, vice-presider Miss M.G. Nicolson, secretary; Mrs C.S. Miller, treasure Mrs M. Morrison, convener of the handicrafts; Miss Doull, show secretary; Miss C. Davidson, assistant sho secretary.

Her Majesty spent some time inspecting the work on vie and told Mrs Millikin that she was surprised to see such high standard of craftmanship in the far North.

Adjacent to the W.R.I. tent was the Red Cross Society caravan, where four V.A.D. nurses were on duty if require Here she was met by Lady Murray, president. She mac inquiries regarding recruiting and asked if there was a junic section of the Red Cross in the county. (There is none present).

Those presented were Mrs A.E. Balfour, Scrabste county director; Mrs A.B. Doull, Wick, county secretar Mr James Wares, Wick, county treasurer, and V.A.D.s M M. Bain, Mrs W. Nicolson, Mrs J. Gunn (all Wick) and M Aldridge (Thurso).

Six people were treated for minor cuts.

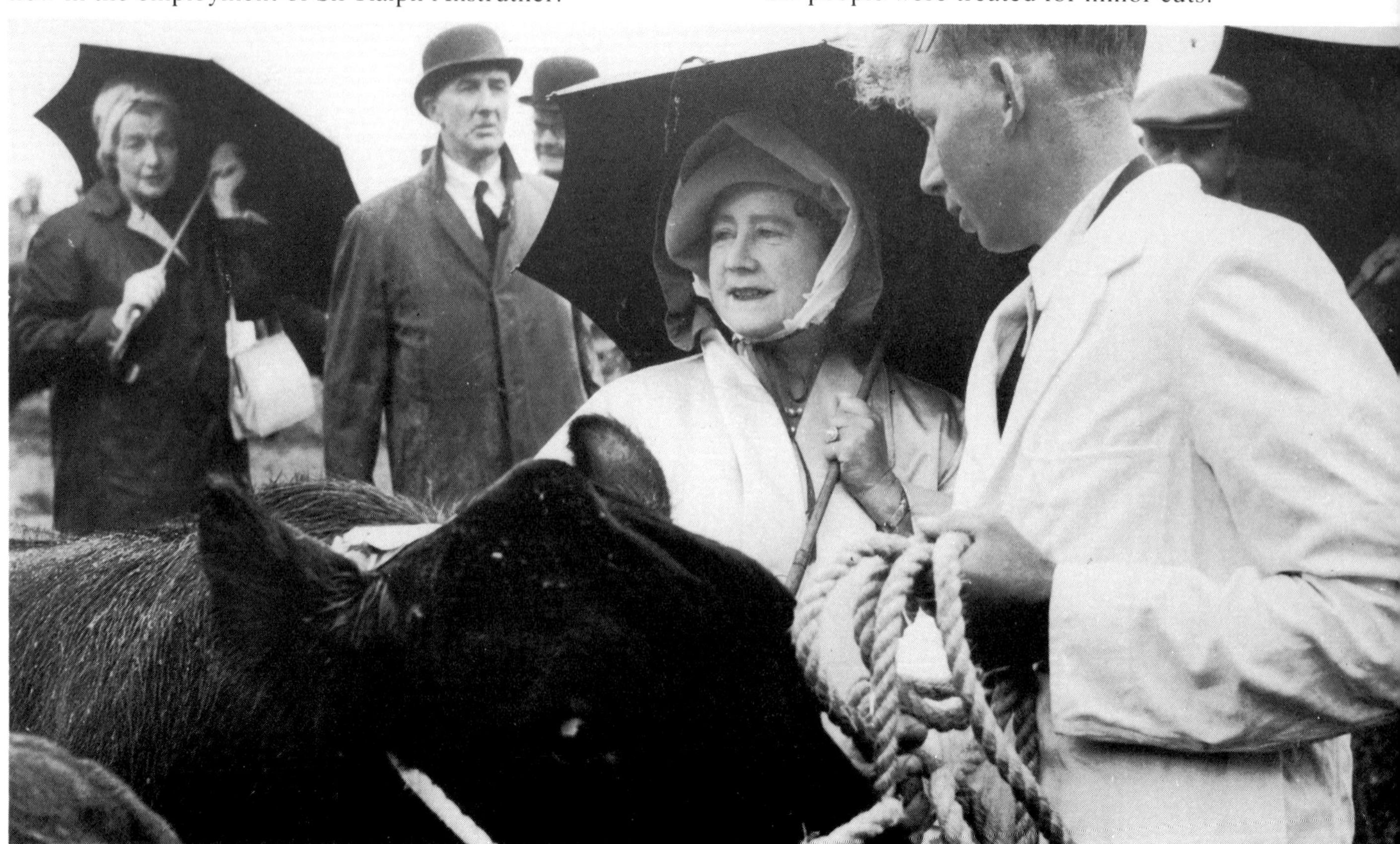

The Queen Mother admires one of the exhibits at the Caithness County Show. She later amused the crowd by emptying all the water out of one of the trophies before handing it over.

Queen Mother visits Scrabster

Thurso Lifeboat Week off to a Royal start

Queen Elizabeth the Queen Mother attended the opening f Thurso's Lifeboat Week at Scrabster on Monday 6th ugust. Thousands of people thronged the quays. A varied rogramme was held in brilliant weather. Her Majesty was et by ex-Provost John Sinclair, chairman of the Thurso ranch of the Lifeboat Institution, and she was presented with a bouquet by Mrs Gertrude Blyth, vice-president of the Ladies' Guild, who was introduced by Miss Louise Kennedy, the president.

The lifeboat was launched from the slipway to go to a "casualty". Thurso Life-Saving Company gave a demonstration in the harbour with the breeches buoy.

ifeboat Fete Scrabster: The Queen Mother was concerned that the two girls (pictured in bathing costumes above) who had been demonstrating a lifesaving device, should be feeling the cold.

The Queen Mother admiring the garden produce stall at the Lifeboat Fete, Scrabster.

Her Majesty greets the people

Coxswain Angus Macintosh and his men are presented to Her Majesty

The Queen Mother gives a flower from her bouquet to a French student in the crowd

Canisbay minister, Rev. George Bell, greets the Queen Mother

The Queen Mother with Miss Louise Kennedy (left) President of the Thurso Branch of the lifeboat institution and ex-provost Sinclair, chairman at Scrabster Harbour. In the distance, the St Ola sails for Orkney.

Queen Mother visits Glass Factory

Queen Elizabeth the Queen Mother, spent almost three quarters of an hour at the Wick Glass Factory on Friday 10 August. It was a private visit. Her Majesty, who had motored from the Castle of Mey, was accompanied by Sir Ralph Anstruther and Lady Fermoy. She was met by the Hon. Robin M. Sinclair, managing director, who presented Mr D. Obroin, designer and technical adviser, and Mr Simon Fraser, secretary.

The Queen Mother, who saw the whole manufacturing process from start to finish, showed great interest in the work and as she went round the factory she spoke to many of the staff.

Before leaving, the Royal visitor was presented by M Sinclair with a paperweight — a real work of art, beautiful designed and in brilliant colours — Mille Fiore (a millio flowers). It was one of six specially made the previous day, s that Her Majesty could make her own choice.

It was made by Mr Paul Ysart, a 58-year-old Spania from Barcelona, who is the glasshouse supervisor in th factory. He is one of a family who have been glassmakers f generations. He came to Edinburgh as a boy with his fath and became an apprentice glassmaker. For 41 years he wa employed in the Perth factory and took up his prese appointment a few months ago.

The Queen Mother is introduced to Mr D. O'Broin, designer and technical adviser to Caithness Glass, by The Hon Robin M Sinclair (centre)

Her Majesty showed great interest in the various manufacturing processes during her tour of the factory

The Queen Mother admiring some of the products, including paperweights, one of which she accepted as a gift

The Queen Mother watching the finishing machine in operation.

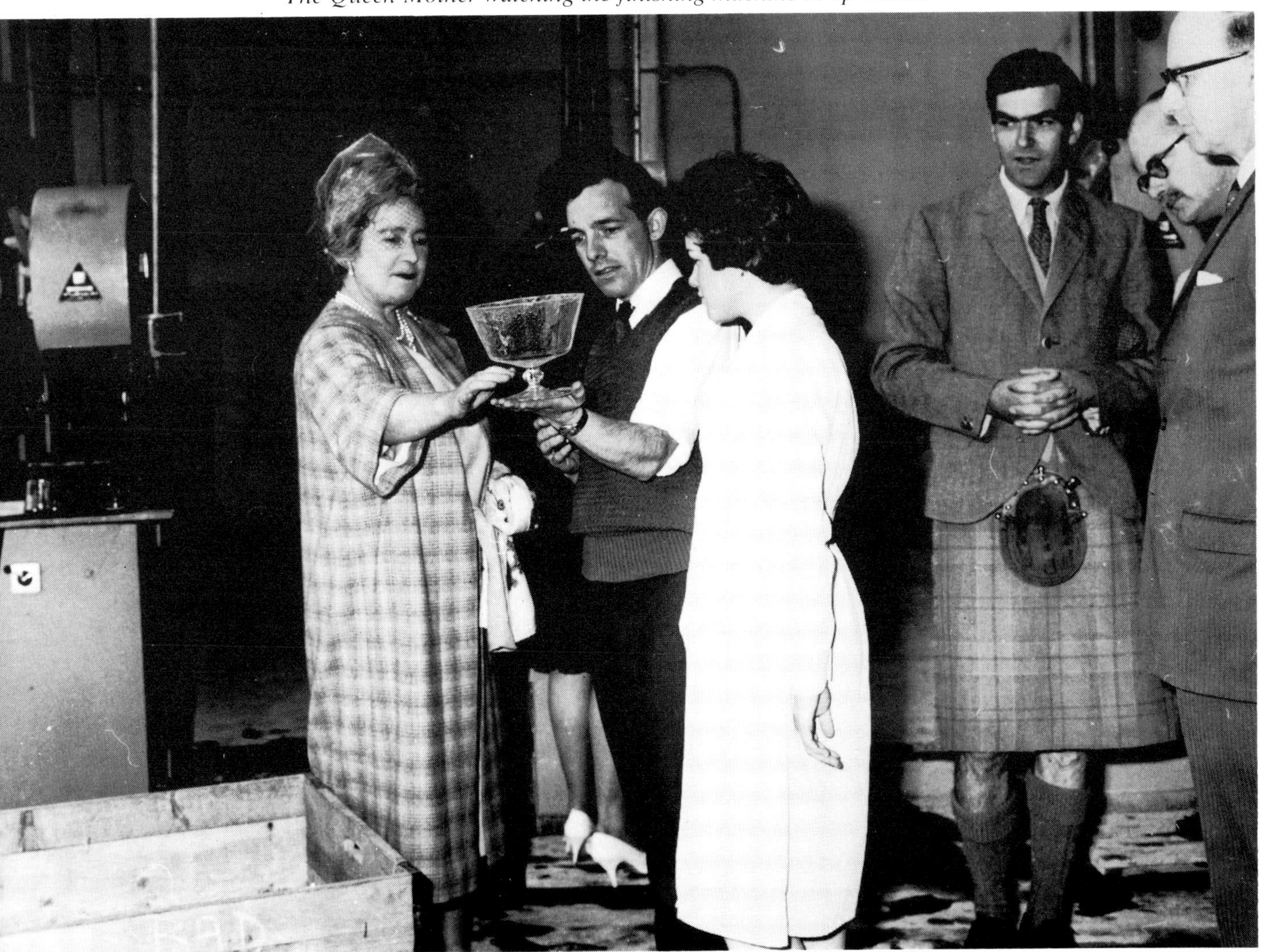

Mr Young, manager, and a member of the staff showing Her Majesty one of the products

MAY 1963

Duke of Edinburgh's day in the North

Visit to Wick Glass Factory and Brora Mine

At the close of a one-day visit to Caithness and Sutherland on Wednesday 1st May, when he toured Wick's new glass factory and the Brora colliery and brick works, the Duke of Edinburgh said it had been one of the most encouraging and interesting he had ever spent inspecting industrial enterprises in Britain.

A large number of people gathered at the Airport to see the Royal visitor arrive. Most of them had walked from the town.

The plane — a Heron of the Queen's Flight — touched down shortly after 10.30. The Duke was at the controls. Before this, there had been several heavy rainshowers and the weather at the time looked far from promising.

Prince Philip was welcomed by Brigadier Sir Keith Murray, Vice-Lieutenant of Caithness and Convener of the County.

Those presented to the Duke were Sheriff Harald R. Leslie, Sheriff-Principal of Caithness, Sutherland, Orkney and Zetland; Mr John L. Russell, county clerk and clerk to the Lieutenancy; Mr John M. Rollo, chairman of the Highland Fund; Mr G.T. Stanley, airport commandant; and Mr John W. Georgeson, chief constable.

Drawn up on the tarmac was a guard of honour — 12 members of the Wick Sea Cadet Corps — under Sub-Lieutenant D. Bogle. In addition there was a full muster of the rest of the Corps, numbering about 50 boy and girl cadets. They were standing at attention a short distance the left of the guard of honour under the charge of Lie W.F. Crummey, who was accompanied by Lieut. J. Macad and Sub-Lieut. D. Sutherland.

Duke Catches Fainting Boy

Prince Philip had just finished inspecting the guard whe on an impluse, he decided to inspect the others as well.

As he walked in front of the line one of the boys sway forward in a faint. Quick as a flash, the Duke turned a caught him in his arms before he could fall. The boy — 1 year-old James Miller, 52 Leith Walk — was then assisted his companions until a woman spectator, Mrs Moi Swanson, who also happens to reside in Leith Walk, r forward to help. She is a part-time nurse in the Henders Memorial Home. Others, including Mrs Crummey, al went to the boy's aid and he was taken to the Airport Fi Service headquarters, where he got a hot drink and so recovered.

Then there was a thoughtful gesture by Prince Philip, w told the officers to dismiss the boys as there might be mo rain. Just afterwards there was another heavy downpour a the Cadets took cover.

From the Airport, the Duke proceeded by car to the Tov House, passing through cheering crowds on the way.

Prince Philip at the controls of a Heron of the Queen's Flight, arrives at Wick Airport for a one day visit to Caithness an Sutherland

On Parade: Inspecting the Guard of Honour — members of Wick Sea Cadet Corps at the Airport

May 1963

Duke accepts unique gift

At the Town House he met Provost William Dunnett, who presented the town clerk, Mr William C. Hogg, and Bailies David S. Falconer and William G. Mowat.

After inspecting a guard of honour provided by the Wick Air Training Corps, under the charge of Flt.-Lt. J.T. Gunn and W.O. J.D.M. Watt, the Royal visitor entered the Town House where the members of the Council and officials were presented. He had coffee and, before leaving for the Glass Factory, he signed the visitors' book.

On the route to the factory, which is situated in Harrow Road, opposite the east side of the Bignold Park, crowds of people stood.

At the factory the visitor was met by Mr Rollo, who presented the Hon. Robin M. Sinclair, managing director, Colonel H.R. Hildreth, director, and Mr D. Obroin, technical director.

The Duke was then shown over the premises by Mr Sinclair and saw the whole process of glass manufacture from start to finish. The factory, a new, local venture established 18 months ago to provide work mainly for young people and to show what is possible in the North, now employs over 50 people, including 20 apprentices.

At the start of his tour round, the first person he stopped to speak to was 58-year-old Mr Bruce Walton, a batch mixer, who previously worked as a baker and is a former well-known local footballer. Looking at a piece of green glass which Mr Walton showed him, the Duke asked: "Is this used for making beer bottles?" Mr Walton replied that it was not, but was used for making a product known as sooty glass.

Accompanying the party on the tour was Mr Paul Ysart, foreman supervisor in the glassworks, who has been employed at the factory for the past year. A native of Spain, he has been a glassworker in this country since his youth, and before coming north was 40 years in Perth, to which he went from Edinburgh.

Just before leaving the premises the Duke was presented with a gift of Caithness glass — a beautiful suite of 19 pieces, including a decanter which was engraved with Prince Philip's coat of arms.

Named Scaraben suite, it was designed, made and engraved by Mr Obroin.

The gift was presented by 24-year-old Miss Laura Mackay, manageress.

Mr Obroin, who finished the suite the previous night, said it was engraved by the copper wheel method. Describing the suite, he said: "It is a unique development in glass; it is black and white. There is nothing like it anywhere."

Mr Obroin, who designed the factory and the layout, said the Duke was surprised at the progress which had been made in apprentice training in such a short time. "Mo of our apprentices are two yea ahead of other glass workers. W had no option but to push them c because we started with loc labour."

The Duke left the works with memento of his visit — his signa ture on the inside of a sweet dis reading: "Philip, May 1, 1963".

From Wick the Duke set off f Brora by car. On his arrival at th Marine Hotel, Brora Pipe Ban under PipeMajor Cairn Suthe land, were playing a new marc composed for the occasion: "Th Welcome of the Duke of Edi burgh to Brora."

Prince Philip enjoys a joke with one of the workers

Royal Visitor at Caithness Art Show

Her Majesty viewing some of the paintings, accompanied by Sheriff D.B. Keith (right) and Major J.B. Simpson (left).

Queen Elizabeth the Queen Mother visited the annual art show held in Thurso by the Society of Caithness Artists. She was welcomed by the society president, Major James B. Simpson, Wick, and spent three-quarters of an hour viewing the exhibits accompanied by Major Simpson and Sheriff D.B. Keith, Kirkwall, a native of Thurso who is one of the leading members of the Society.

The exhibition closed on Saturday 17th August. Attendances were up to the usual and the exhibits were favourably commented upon by visitors.

Winner of the lucky ticket in a free gift draw, costing 6d and valid for any picture of the winner's choice up to £10 10s, was Miss J.I. Taylor, Gerston, Halkirk.

At Canisbay Church

The Queen Mother attended the noon service in Canisbay Old Church on Sunday 18th August. She wore a light blue coat and hat to match. Along with her were Commander C.G. Vyner and Lady Doris Vyner, of the House of the Northern Gate; Lady Fermoy, Lady-in-Waiting; Sir Ralph Anstruther, Treasurer, and Captain David MacMicking, Equerry.

Her Majesty was welcomed by the minister, Rev. George Bell. There was a large congregation. A number of people saw the Royal visitor arrive and there was a much larger crowd at the church entrance when she left.

Visit to Thurso Shop

The Queen Mother paid a visit to Thurso on Tuesday and made some purchases at the shop of J. Miller Calder, house furnishers, Traill Street.

The Queen Mother returned south yesterday (Thursday), flying from Wick to Dyce, Aberdeenshire, in a Heron of the Queen's Flight. She is joining the Royal Family at Balmoral.

Royal Visit to the North

Rousing welcome for the Queen and the Duke Enthusiastic scenes at Wick and Thurso

Her Majesty the Queen and H.R.H. the Duke of Edinburgh received a rousing welcome from thousands of spectators in Wick and Thurso on Wednesday 24th June and yesterday, Thursday 25th June, during the course of their three-day visit to the North of Scotland when they carried out a number of engagements in ideal weather conditions — the warmest spell enjoyed in the North this summer.

It was the Queen's first official visit to Caithness, althoug she had spent a few hours in the county on two previou occasions — private visits to the Castle of Mey when th Queen Mother was in residence — the first being in 195 Her Majesty had never before been in the Royal Burgh Wick, of which the Queen Mother is a Free Burges Throughout the visit, everyone was impressed with th delightful informality of the Royal visitors.

Her Majesty arrives at Wick Airport where she was welcomed by the Hon. Robin M. Sinclair, Deputy Lieutenant of the Coun (left).

The organisation of the Caithness visit — spread over two ays — was excellent. It placed heavy commitments on the ounty police. Traffic was well controlled and everything ent smoothly. The cheering crowds were able to see the Royal visitors all along the official routes and from many antage points.

A large crowd, consisting mainly of schoolchildren, reeted the Queen and Duke of Edinburgh when they rrived at Wick Airport — seven minutes later than the cheduled time — on Wednesday afternoon.

Her Majesty was the first to step out of the bright red Heron aircraft. A loud burst of cheering marked her exit rom the plane and she paused slightly to wave to the happy rowd.

The Queen was dressed in a coat of deep turquoise blue wool, cut on easy fitting lines, with dress to match. Her hat was a wide-brimmed straw of a lighter shade than her coat. Her bag, shoes and gloves were grey and she had a brooch pinned on her coat.

Prince Philip, dressed in a dark grey suit with a black and ed striped tie and brown trilby hat, followed the Queen on o the tarmac runway where they were met by the Hon. Mr Sinclair.

Scottish Secretary

Also in the Royal party were the right Honourable Mr Michael Nobel, Secretary of State for Scotland; The Countess of Leicester (Lady-in-Waiting); Lieutenant-Colonel the Honourable Sir Martin Charteris (Assistant Private Secretary to Her Majesty); Lord Plunket (Equerry-n-Waiting to Her Majesty); and Squadron Leader Check-etts (Equerry to His Royal Highness).

The Deputy Lieutenant of the county then presented his wife, the Hon. Mrs Robin Sinclair; Mr Harald Leslie, Q.C., Sheriff of Caithness, Sutherland, Orkney and Shetland; Mrs Leslie; Colonel J.J. Robertson, Deputy Lieutenant: Mr Walter Sinclair, Thurso, County Convener; Mr John L. Russell, county clerk and clerk to the Lieutenancy; Mrs Russell; Mr E.M. Hunter, airport commandant; and Mr John W. Georgeson, chief constable.

Minutes later, as Her Majesty stepped into the wine-coloured Rolls Royce, the eager spectators flowed over the barriers to catch an extra glimpse of their radiant Queen. Although the sky was slightly overcast, it was one of the warmest days in the north this summer, with temperatures in the mid-sixties.

From the airport, the Royal cars drove through Hill Avenue and on to the main north road via Castletown to Thurso. At the small villages and hamlets on the route, children were out in force with their flags and decorations and many people watched the small procession from various vantage points.

At Thurso

At Thurso, youth organisations packed the High Street outside the Town Hall, where Provost Miss Isabella Cormack was presented by the Hon. Mr Sinclair. Miss Cormack then presented Mr James S. Abernethy, town clerk, and Mrs Abernethy.

Inside the Council Room, members of Thurso Town Council were presented to the Queen and Duke. There were: Bailies Dr W.R.N. Sutherland; Daniel Mackay, and David K. Sutherland; Dean of Guild, Douglas P. Shaw; Mr David Allan, burgh chamberlain; Mr David A. Stewart, burgh surveyor; and Mr Hugh S. Macdonald, burgh architect.

Before leaving the Town Hall, Her Majesty and Prince Philip signed the visitors book and several portraits. On the steps of the Hall, little six-year-old Camilla Sinclair, daughter of Deputy Lieutenant, presented a bouquet to the Queen.

A Host of Cheering Children.—A typical scene during the tour. Some of the hundreds of school children who greeted the Royal couple when they arrived at Wick Airport at the start of their visit.

At Thurso, the Queen and Duke are welcomed outside the Town Hall by Provost Miss Isabella Cormack

Her Majesty the Queen at Thurso Town Hall after receiving a bouquet from six year old Camilla Sinclair

By four o'clock the Royal party left the centre of the town, travelling slowly through the crowded streets to the modern Technical College.

They were received at the College by the County Convener and those presented were: Provost William F. Dunnett, Wick, Vice-Convener; Mr Thomas W. Pollok, Thurso, chairman of the Education Committee; Mr J. Abrach Mackay, Castletown, chairman of the Accident Prevention Committee; Mr Ian Stewart, Reisgill, chairman of the Roads Committee; Mr Hugh R. Stewart, director of education; Mr J. Kennedy, county treasurer; Mr William Wilson, county architect; Mr James C. McIntosh, county engineer; Dr C.N. Minto, medical officer of health; Dr R.H. Roberts, principal of Thurso Technical College; and Mr Roy R. Matthews, director at Dounreay Atomic Station.

While Her Majesty, accompanied by the County Convener and the college principal, visited the County Industrial Exhibition and went by lift to the top floor of the magnificent new building, the Duke of Edinburgh, with the Vice-Convener and the Dounreay director, met members of the Institute of Physics and the Physical Society (Scottish branch) at a conference in the hall.

His Royal Highness also visited the Industrial Exhibition in the library. Among the larger industries represented were Caithness Glass, Halkirk Plastics, Caithness Cheese, Wick Knitwear and the Dounreay Apprentices Scheme.

The Queen and the Duke then joined again for tea in the Gymnasium where the Hon. Mr Sinclair presented the following: Rev. A.F. Andrew, Halkirk, Moderator of the Caithness Church of Scotland Presbytery; Mrs A.E. Balfour, Thurso, county director of the British Red Cross Society; Mrs G. Blyth, Thurso, lifeboat guild; Captain J. Budge, Thurso, Boys' Brigade; Mrs M. Glass, Wick, W.V.S. Darby and Joan Club, Major George Green, Crossroads, chairman, T.A. and A.F. association for Caithness; Mrs Jessamine Harmsworth, Thrumster, president, Caithness Federation W.R.I.; Miss M.M. Henderson, matron, Dunbar Hospital, Thurso; Mr J.A. Gore-Browne Henderson, Wick, county commissioner of scouts; Mrs K.I. Duff-Dunbar, Wick, former county commissioner of guides; Miss L.M. Kennedy, Thurso, lifeboat guild; Miss A.A. Lindsay, Thurso, former commissioner of guides; Dr J.L. Macaulay, Lybster, general practitioner; Mr Ian Mair, Thurso Youth Club Leader; Mr William Manson, Thurso, retired postman; Miss J. Munro, matron, Forse House, Lybster; Mr David Oag, editor, John O'Groat Journal, Wick; Mr A.N. Roxburgh, Wick, surgeon; Miss Rosalind S. Stamp, matron, Town and County Hospital, Wick; Sheriff Substitute Ewen Stewart, Watten; Mrs J. Woollecombe, Wick, county commissioner of guides; and students of the college.

So interesting was the College, that by the time the Royal party left for Scrabster by car, they were a good twenty-five minutes behind schedule. Again the route was packed with onlookers — many with flags — waiting for Her Majesty and Prince Philip to pass.

The Queen is introduced to the welcoming party at Thurso Technical College by the County Convener.

Her Majesty the Queen pictured at The Industrial Exhibition. Among the larger industries represented were, Caithness Glass (Top) and Wick Knitwear (above)

(Top): The Queen in conversation with a representative of Caithness Cheese. (Above): Prince Philip chats to a young apprentice on the Dounreay Apprentices Scheme Stand.

Delighted children and mothers watch the Queen passing

The Brownies (right), wave and cheer as Her Majesty leaves Thurso Technical College accompanied by the County Convener

The departure from Scrabster Harbour.

Her Majesty the Queen and Prince Philip prepare to embark on the Royal barge at Scrabster.

By this time the sun was shining strongly and the crowds in shirt sleeves and bright summer dresses added plenty of colour to the great occasion.

Arriving at Scrabster Pier the county Deputy Lieutenant presented Captain W. Mackenzie, harbourmaster; Mr G.M.B. Henderson, chairman of the Harbour Trust; Mrs Henderson; Commander Alec. Barlow, Admiralty Reactor Test Establishment; Commander J.L. Woollecombe; Lieutenant-Commander F.C. Waterloo, U.S. Navy; Mr Angus MacIntosh, coxswain of Thurso lifeboat; and M G.R. Cullington, commodore of the Pentland Firth Sailin Club.

Hundreds of people had gathered along the waterfront t watch the Queen and the Royal party board the barge whic took them out to the Britannia, anchored in Thurso Bay.

After leaving Thurso Bay later on in the evening, th Royal yacht sailed round the coast and anchored in Sinclai Bay for the night. Many people took advantage of the fine calm evening to drive out and see Britannia.

The Royal Barge leaving Scrabster to take the Royal visitors to the Britannia

The Queen and Duke arrive in Wick by Royal barge

The Queen and Duke enter Wick Harbour in the Royal barge with escorts.

JUNE 1964

Visit to the Royal Burgh

On Thursday, 25th June the whole of Wick and district seemed to have turned out along the Braehead, Smith Terrace, Bexley Terrace, Harbour Terrace and the harbour itself, as the Queen and Duke landed from the Royal barge at precisely five minutes past ten.

Her Majesty wore a light amber wool coat with a small fitting hat of darker amber velvet loops. Her shoes, bag and gloves were of a mink shade.

They were met at the steps of the south quay by the Hon. Mr Sinclair, the County Convener and Provost Dunnett. Those presented to the Queen and Duke were: the Provost's wife, Mrs Wm. F. Dunnett; Mr Wm. C. Hogg, town clerk, and Mrs Hogg; Mr Neil Stewart, harbourmaster and coxswain of Wick lifeboat; and Mr David Dunnett, chairman of Wick Harbour Trust.

Amid deafening cheering, the Royal car made its way along the quays, thronged with people, to Martha Terrace, across the Service Bridge and into the town centre.

It travelled up High Street, Bridge Street, past the Town Hall, across the bridge and arrived at the Assembly Rooms via Cliff Road and Sinclair Terrace, all of which were very gaily decorated.

The Queen and Prince Philip entered the community centre at the Malcolm Street door and within the David Mowat Room, the Provost invited Her Majesty and His Royal Highness to sign the visitors' book and portraits.

In the concert hall itself, representatives from all the loc organisations,the Town Council and their wives and officia had assembled.

Guests Presented

The Hon. Mr Sinclair first presented Sir David Robertso Member of Parliament for Caithness and Sutherland, an Lady Robertson, and then Provost Dunnett presented th following:

Bailies George Bruce, Kenneth M. Gunn and George C Fraser; Dean of Guild, George Gunn; Police Judges Davi S. Falconer and John Macleod; Mr James Ward, burg chamberlain; Mr Alex. S. Begg, burgh surveyor; and M John McDonald, water engineer (all Wick Town Council Mr C. Donaldson, area manager, Ministry of Pensions an National Insurance; Mr James Wares, treasurer, Wic Branch of the Royal National Lifeboat Institution; Mrs A.E Doull, secretary, Caithness Branch of the British Red Cros Society, ex-Provost J.H. Leishman, Civil Defence Grou Controller; Rev. W. Nethercote Scott, minister of Wick Ol Parish Church; Mr J. Bruce, president, Wick Tow Improvements Association; Mrs A. Eaton, secretary, Wic Playing Field Association; and Mr James Bremner, fishe man.

Her Majesty and Prince Philip step ashore at Wick, after the Royal barge lands at the South Quay.

A Rolls Royce reception for the Queen and Prince Philip at Wick Harbour.

The Queen signs a portrait of herself during the visit to the Wick Assembly Rooms.

The Royal couple then walked round the splendid hall chatting occasionally to members of the different youth organisations of the county. The party took a short walk through to the Games Room and watched an exhibition given by Wick Judo Club.

The Club's secretary, Mr Brian Easy, was presented and talked with Prince Philip as the members went through their paces. Bailie Bruce was in attendance.

Her Majesty was first to notice the only girl among the white-robed competitors, 12-year-old Elizabeth Richard, 6 Hill Avenue, Wick, who recently gained the 2nd Mon belt. Those taking part were: Alan Clarke, Raymond Tait, Richard Lapwood, Brian Harness, David Walker, Stuart Thomson, Joe Ewing, Allan Doull, Elizabeth Richard, Paul Easy, Malcolm Cook, Steven Webster, Brian Cornwell, Stewart Gunn, Russell Dunnett and Tommy Farmer.

Gifts Presented

Returning to the hall, the Queen accepted a set of 12 Caithness-made sherry glasses, a gift from the Town Council. The glasses, which had a simple black and crystal design, were from the Scaraben range produced locally at the Caithness Glass Factory, Harrowhill.

Her Majesty was then asked to accept a gift from the young people of the county for Prince Charles — a table model of a Wick fishing boat. Making the presentation was Boys' Brigade Corporal James Gunn of the 1st Wick Company, who recently won a double honour with the Queen's Badge — the highest B.B. award — and the Duke of Edinburgh's award at the silver level.

Corporal Gunn, who is 17, is a pupil of Wick High School. No more fitting youth representative could have been chosen to make the presentation. It is no mean achievement for any boy to gain the coveted Duke of Edinburgh's awa and the Queen's Badge but it is a remarkable double hono for James who suffered for a number of years from a physic handicap. He is a keen sportsman and plays at left back f Wick Groats F.C. James is a son of Mr and Mrs John Gun County Cafe, High Street.

The boat — a 12 inch made-to-scale model — represents herring fishing vessel of the sailing days, the Ben Aige (recalling the Zulu type). It was made by 70-year-old retire marine engineer, Mr Alex. D. Manson, West Bank Avenue, Wick, a native of Keiss. Mr Manson's father, th late Mr S. Manson, was a herring fisherman, sailing in th New Vine (WK 995), a "Fifie" built craft.

Mr A.D. Manson, who sailed as an engineer (first-class was employed with the Currie Line and Salvensons. O leaving the sea he worked as an engineer in the Wic Electricity Power Station. While he loves to build mod boats, he is also a talented artist — ships, seascapes an landscapes.

Disabled Ex-Servicemen

Before leaving the Assembly Rooms, the Queen stoppe to be presented to several disabled ex-servicemen in th lobby of the former Pulteneytown Academy.

Outside, at the junction of Malcolm Street and Sincla Terrace, the Royal couple spoke to veteran Pipe-Majo James Christie, and one of the members of the Wick Girls Pipe Band.

As the County Convener, the Provost and the Hon. Robi Sinclair took their leave, the Girls' Pipe Band played out fitting ending to the short but enjoyable Royal tour o Caithness. The gleaming Rolls proceeded slowly down packed Sinclair Terrace, turned left into Cliff Road an Francis Street and left the flag-waving inhabitants of Wic behind it as it journeyed south for Helmsdale — its next stop

Provost Dunnett presents a gift of Caithness Glass on behalf of the Royal Burgh

The Queen meets representatives of one of the many local organisations.

The Queen sees members of the Wick Judo Club who gave a display in the Assembly Rooms

Her Majesty stops to greet a member of the Sea Cadets.

Cpl James Gunn, 1st B.B., presents to Her Majesty a model of a Wick herring fishing boat as a gift for the Prince Charles from th county, on behalf of the youth of Caithness.

Her Majesty the Queen escorted by Provost Dunnett, leaves the Assembly Rooms, followed by Prince Philip and The Hon. Robin Sinclair

The Queen and Prince Philip with members of the Wick Pipe Band. Their leader pipe major James Christie stands by.

As the Royal pair leave the Assembly Rooms, they respond to the cheers from the large crowd.

Queen Mother On Holiday

Queen Elizabeth the Queen Mother arrives at Wick Airport

Queen Elizabeth the Queen Mother is on holiday at the Castle of Mey. She flew from London to Wick on Saturday in an Avro Andover of the Queen's Flight. A north westerly gale was blowing when the plane touched down at Wick shortly after 3 o'clock. Her Majesty was accompanied by Lady Fermoy, Lady-in-Waiting.

A small group of people saw the Royal visitor arrive. She wore a light grey coat with hat to match and carried a fur stole.

The Lord Lieutenant of Caithness, Brigadier Sir Keith Murray, sent the following telegram to Her Majesty:

"On behalf of the people of Caithness I send Your Majesty loyal greetings and warmest good wishes on the occasion of Your Majesty's birthday."

Her Majesty's reply read: "Please convey to the people of Caithness my warm thanks for the message of good wishes. I am so happy to be spending my birthday in the beloved place."

Wick Flower Show

For their fifteenth annual flower show held in the Assembly Rooms, Wick and District Horticultural Society were honoured with a visit from Her Majesty Queen Elizabeth the Queen Mother. She arrived at the show shortly after four o'clock accompanied by Lady Doris Vyner, Dunnet, and Mrs J. Mulholland, Lady-in-Waiting.

She wore a fine wool coat in royal blue with hat to match and black accessories.

Mr D.M. Sutherland, secretary, welcomed Her Majesty, and with Mr James Begg, president, escorted the royal party on a tour of the stalls. Also present were honorary presidents of the Society, Mrs Kenneth Duff-Dunbar, Hempriggs House, who opened the show, and Sheriff Ewen Stewart, with Mrs Stewart.

The Queen Mother delighted the large crowd with the typical informality of her visit. She spent over half-an-hour inspecting the exhibits and had a word for many of the onlookers as well as for the exhibitors.

One of those to whom she spoke was Mrs Florence Ra whose husband came to Wick from Arbroath as assista head postmaster, Mrs Rae's two-year-old son Stephen ha fallen asleep in her arms as she watched the Royal visitor g by. The Queen Mother asked whether or not he w enjoying the show, to which Mrs Rae replied: "I am sorry, h has fallen asleep." "It is a good thing because he must b tired," remarked the Queen Mother.

Her Majesty also spoke to Miss Beatrice Simpson, th Flower Centre, Wick who had arranged an extreme impressive display in the hall, and to representatives o Messrs D. & W. Croll, Dundee, who have had a stand at th show for a number of years.

"Very Creditable"

After her tour of the exhibition she described the numbe and quality of entries as "very creditable". She left th Assembly Rooms just after 4.30 to the applause of th crowd.

Her Majesty arrving at the Assembly Rooms, Wick, for the Fifteenth Annual Flower Show.

Mey Sheep Dog Trials Success

Mey Sheep Dog Trials Association held its annual event this year a month later than usual and it was so successful that it is likely that they will stick to a date in August.

Entries were up on last year, gate drawings also rose, and with a largely-attended dance to round off the day, the organisers were well satisfied with the day's result.

To crown their success they had a Royal visitor at the trials. Queen Elizabeth the Queen Mother had accepted an invitation to attend. She arrived at the ground in a Land Rover, and was accompanied by Commander C.G. Vyner, Lady Doris Vyner, Mrs J. Mulholland, Lady-in-Waiting, Sir Martin Gilliat, Secretary, and Captain David MacMicking, Equerry.

Her Majesty was welcomed by Mr A. Kennedy, Tresdale, president of the Society, who was accompanied by the secretary, Mr Wm. Leitch. Mr Kennedy, who is also this year's president of the Caithness Agricultural Society, offered his congratulations to the Queen Mother on her success at the county show at which she won the supreme championship and reserve award for North Country Cheviot sheep.

Although the weather was dull and cool, the Queen Mother stayed for almost two hours watching the competition, in which more than 50 handlers took part, including some of the country's leading men of national and international fame.

The Royal visitor and party saw a splendid exhibition by Mr Raymond Macpherson, Dalangwell, the judge, during an interval in the contest. His display with three dogs was a masterly example by an expert handler.

A Masterly Display: Mr Raymond MacPherson with his three sheep dogs, gave a splendid exhibition at the Mey Sheep Dog Trials. The Queen Mother looks on with evident delight

A carefree afternoon at the Mey Sheepdog Trials

Queen Elizabeth the Queen Mother at Wick Airport before returning south at the end of her three week holiday in Caithness

Queen Mother visits local antique shop

Queen Elizabeth the Queen Mother attended the noon service in Canisbay Old Church on Sunday. The service was conducted by the minister, Rev. George Bell, who welcomed Her Majesty on arrival.

The Queen Mother was accompanied by her niece, Miss Elizabeth Elphinstone, Lady Elizabeth Basset, Lady-in-Waiting, Major Raymond Seymour and Captain David MacMicking, Equerries.

There was a fairly large congregation, about a dozen people saw the Royal visitor arrive at the church. She wore a pink coat with hat to match.

On Monday the Queen Mother went shopping in Thurso, making purchases in Miller Calder's furnishing premises and in the Ship's Wheel, an antique shop.

Her Majesty returned to Birkhall, her Deeside residence. She travelled in her private car from the Castle of Mey.

The picture reproduced shows the Queen Mother at Wick Airport when she arrived last week.

The St. Ola passenger ship on her way to berth, passing the Britannia at anchor

Royal Family Land At Scrabster

Visit to Queen Mother

The Queen and the Duke of Edinburgh along with the Royal family, spent about five hours in Caithness on Sunday when they came ashore at Scrabster to visit the Queen Mother who was on holiday at the Castle of Mey.

They landed from the Royal yacht Britannia, which was on her way from the west coast to Aberdeen. The Britannia put into Thurso bay in the forenoon, and the visitors came ashore in the Royal barge.

News of the Queen's impending visit soon spread and by noon the pier at Scrabster was crowded with people, including many holidaymakers. The weather was fine, with a grey sky and a cool wind.

The Queen Mother had travelled in her private car from Mey to welcome her guests. She was accompanied by the Hon. Mrs J. Mulholland, Lady-in-Waiting, Sir Martin Gilliat, Secretary, and Captain David MacMicking, Equerry.

There were loud cheers from the crowd as the Queen and the rest of the party came alongside the pier steps anc ascended to the quay. They were officially welcomed by thc Hon. Robin M. Sinclair, Thurso East, Vice-Lieutenant o Caithness.

They had lunch with the Queen Mother and later spen some time on the beach below the Castle.

Apart from her official visit to the county last year wher she carried out public engagements at Wick and Thurso, this was the Queen's third informal visit to Caithness since 1955 And it was the informality of this visit that impressed thc crowds —both piers at the harbour entrance were packec with people hours before the Royal family re-embarked or the Britannia shortly after 5 p.m.

The Queen Mother returned to Scrabster to see her guests depart. The Britannia sailed soon after the visitors were back on board, and the Queen Mother travelled back to Mey.

The Queen Mother greets the Queen and the Duke of Edinburgh, Princess Anne and Prince Andrew at Scrabster

ler Majesty the Queen chatting with the Queen Mother on the quayside, while Prince Andrew looks on as a spectator snaps a shot.

A smiling Queen greets Sir Martin Gilliat, secretary to the Queen Mother.

Prince Andrew viewing the scene with evident delight.

Queen Elizabeth the Queen Mother leaves Wick Airport at the end of her summer holiday at the Castle of Mey

A Birthday Portrait of the Queen Mother with her favourite corgis Billy and Bee in the privacy of Her Caithness Home

Caithness in Pictures

"It is a delight to me that I now have a home in Caithness, a county of such great beauty, combining as it does the peace and tranquility of an open and uncrowded countryside with the rugged glory of a magnificent coastline — the remote detachment of country villages with the busy and independent life of your market towns."

This extract from Queen Elizabeth the Queen Mother's reply on receiving the Freedom of the Royal Burgh of Wick in 1956 may well have been inspired by the sights of Caithness — similar to those illustrated overleaf — captured by John Adams on a journey through the northernmost county in the early 1950s, leading from the Ord, via Berriedale, Dunbeath, Lybster, Wick, John O'Groats, Dunnet and Thurso to the Kyle of Tongue.

The Strath, Berriedale, Caithness.

The Old Smithy at Berriedale — bears many trophies of the shoot.

Berriedale village — nestling in the glen at the foot of Berriedale Brae. This district abounds with deer and is part of the estate of the Duke of Portland.

The village of Dunbeath.

The Portland Arms Hotel at Lybster — provides a welcome stopping place for travellers proceeding north.

Vhaligoe Bay and the 365 steps at Ulbster — where history tells that when fishermen of days long ago landed their catch, their wives carried the herring in baskets up the steps to the main road, thence walked the eight miles to market at Wick.

'ishing vessels in Wick Harbour — fishing, particularly herring fishing, was once the premier industry of Wick and although agriculture has now replaced it as the main industry, fishing is still carried on substantially.

Bridge Street, Wick — this is the County Town of Caithness.

Herring gutting at Wick.

Landing and salting herring at Wick.

Sinclair and Girnigoe Castles, Wick — date back to the time of the Earl of Caithness of 1638 and form a well known Caithness landmark which can be seen for miles on the way to John O'Groats from Wick.

Noss Head and Lighthouse, Wick.

The last house in Britain and the Hotel, at John O'Groats.

John O'Groats Post Office.

Dunnet Bay — where the fine sands and mighty rollers can be seen en route from John O'Groats to Thurso.

Thurso — the northernmost town in Scotland.

Scrabster Harbour near Thurso.

The Stacks of Duncansby — at John O'Groats.

Thurso Castle

Historical Buildings, Thurso (from left to right): Old St. Peter's Church; The Old Turnpike; New St. Peter's Church.

Dounreay Experimental Atomic Reactor Establishment, Caithness.

The M.V. St. Ola, at Scrabster Harbour.

Loch Shurrery near Reay — the "Scarabens" which include Ben Morven, can be seen in the background.

Ben Hope and the Kyle of Tongue — this lovely view can be seen as one leaves Caithness by the West Coast route.

"Britannia" at Scrabster Harbour.

Interior Old Canisbay Church — between Mey and John O'Groats.

Pigeons Cave, Duncansby, John O'Groats.